with

TEEN
SUICIDE

James M. Murphy, M. D.

THE ROSEN PUBLISHING GROUP, INC./NEW YORK

Published in 1999 by The Rosen Publishing Group, Inc.
29 East 21st Street, New York, NY 10010

Cover Photo by Simca Isrealian

First Edition

Library of Congress Cataloging-in-Publication Data
Murphy, James M., M.D.
    Coping with teen suicide / James M. Murphy, M.D.
        p.   cm. — (Coping)
    Includes bibliographical references and index.
    Summary: Explains the causes and consequences of suicide and suggests ways of dealing with problems, preventing suicide, and coping with the suicide of a loved one.
    ISBN 0-8239-2824-1
    1. Teenagers—Suicidal Behavior—United States—Juvenile literature. 2. Suicide—United States—Juvenile literature. 3. Suicide—United States—Prevention Juvenile literature. [1. Suicide.] I. Title. II. Title: Teen Suicide. III. Series.
    HV6546.M87 1999
    362.88'0835'0973—dc20   99-24742
                                                                          CIP
                                                                          AC

Manufactured in the United States of America

About the Author

Jim Murphy is a psychotherapist, who also performs couple, marriage, family and group, and dance therapy in private practice in New York City. He is a faculty member and supervisor at the Blanton-Peale Graduate Institute, which trains psychotherapists, pastoral psychotherapists, and marriage and family therapists. He has an M.D. from New York University and an M.Div. degree from Union Theological Seminary. He is a Life Member of the American Psychiatric Association; a Diplomate in the American Association of Pastoral Counselors; a Clinical Member, Approved Supervisor, and Fellow of the American Association of Marriage and Family Therapy; a Registered Dance Therapist with the Academy of Dance Therapists Registered, and an Ordained Minister of the United Church of Christ. He has worked with many depressed or suicidal young people.

Jim reads and writes poetry and is studying the Chinese language and culture.

Author's Note: The scenarios in this book are based on real people, but the names and circumstances have been changed to protect their identity.

Acknowledgments

I wish to acknowledge the many depressed and suicidal young people who shared their journeys with me in psychotherapy; the supervisors who helped me chart the course and guide my work as I have worked with these young people; the psychotherapists, including my wife, Dr. Thelma Dixon Murphy, and my colleagues, Tyler Bishop and Diane Gregory, who helped me clarify my thinking and who shared their experiences with depressed and suicidal young people; the clinical psychologist Dr. Fred Brown, whose psychological testing helped me identify those young people who were on the path and at the door of suicide and understand their psychodynamics.

I also wish to acknowledge and thank the editors who helped make this book possible: Avis Lang and others who taught me many things about writing, and especially Erica Smith, Senior Editor of Rosen Publishing Group, whose editing stimulated my thinking, helped me form words to convey the ideas, guided the organization of the book, and made it immensely more readable. I thank her and Rosen Publishing for their dedication to helping teenagers cope with issues in their lives.

This book is dedicated:

To those young people who have experienced the depths of human suffering and misery, who have contemplated killing themselves or even started to, and those young people who have survived.

To those therapists who do not avoid or abandon young people because they are depressed or suicidal, who work with them despite professional risks of being blamed if they commit suicide, and who face and cope with the all-too-human reactions of fright of suicide and the dread of death; and

To my wife, Dr. Thelma F. Dixon, whose companionship, support, and positive force for living have been a home base from which to launch the writing of this book.

Contents

Introduction

If you are thinking of taking your own life, think twice. Once you are dead, you don't get a second chance. While you are alive you always have an opportunity to change how you feel, but—to state the obvious—if you are dead, you can't change anything.

This book is about you, the stresses you face, and how you can cope with stress to overcome depression or thoughts of suicide. This book will help you evaluate whether or not you are depressed, on a path to suicide, or at the door of suicide.

This book will also guide you in identifying and solving problems so you can learn how to lead a fulfilling and happy life. If you have been depressed or have had suicidal thoughts in the past, now is a good time to explore some of the things that have contributed to those thoughts and make a plan to avoid the negative influences on your life.

If you think a friend or relative may be suicidal, this book will provide the information you need to help him or her solve problems, change his or her feelings, seek help if needed, and stay alive.

Suicide Is a Major Problem for Teens

Although the rate of suicide in the United States is about twelve suicides per 100,000 people per year, statistics show that the number is even higher for teenagers. Suicide is the second leading cause of death of teenagers, whereas suicide is only the tenth leading cause of death of the general population.

If various kinds of deaths from unnatural causes, such as a fatal disease, are looked at from the point of view of the amount of unlived years of life that result, teenage accidents, suicides, and homicides cause the most unlived years of life of all the deaths from unnatural causes.

Suicide is also a major problem for teenagers not only because many teens actually die by suicide, but because so many teens—unaccounted for in the statistics—are depressed, think of suicide, or attempt suicide. A tremendous amount of pain, unhappiness, and frustration is represented by the numbers of teenagers who are depressed or suicidal.

A Gradual Process Leads to Suicide

When we learn of a suicide reported in the media, it seems to be a sudden, surprising event. An article in *Time* (December 8, 1997) described the suicide of Michael Hutchence, lead singer of INXS, with the headline, "How Could He Have Done It?" The feelings behind a headline like this are very common. Because we don't anticipate someone's suicide, we may think the victim was a well-adjusted, happy person who had everything to live for.

In actuality, suicide is the end result of many things that have happened to a person. It's not as though a voice suddenly commanded someone to kill herself. Instead, during the past six months (and usually during a lifetime), she has had a series of typical thoughts, feelings, and events influencing her to commit suicide. It seems as if the more that is known about a suicidal person, the more that person's suicide is discovered to have followed a lifetime of negative reactions to stress, events, and experiences.

It is possible for you to evaluate whether or not you, or someone you know, is on a path to suicide by comparing your history with those reported here of teenagers who have been suicidal. Their stories reveal many influences, one after another, that gradually led to suicide.

This book also presents options for change. If you are being influenced to be suicidal, this book can help you.

Talk to Someone

If you think about attempting suicide, it is important that you not only read this book but also talk to someone you trust, such as your parents, your teacher, or a religious leader. Don't keep thoughts of suicide to yourself. Even if you think you're all alone and no one cares about your problems, think again. You should never feel so bad about your life that suicide seems like the only answer. And if you can't find someone you feel comfortable talking to, call 1–800–SVA–TEEN. This is a suicide hotline number; the people who answer the phone are caring, trustworthy listeners. They can help you.

Three Major Reasons Not to Kill Yourself

"This too will pass"
Even though you might feel like killing yourself now, your feelings will change and your situation will change.

3

Remember that there was a time when you did not feel like killing yourself. Try to recall how you felt during that period. If you felt that way once before, you can feel that way once again. Nothing is as certain as change, and you can do some things to bring about positive change in your life.

You'll be glad to be alive

Teenagers who have attempted suicide and lived have been very glad a year or two later that they didn't kill themselves. Joe, who had a suicide plan but didn't carry it out, said a year later, "What a nightmare! I can't believe I was thinking of killing myself. I'm lucky I didn't do it, and I'm really glad to be alive."

The pianist Arthur Rubinstein reported in a radio interview that as a young man he had felt very depressed and hopeless and attempted to hang himself, but the rope broke. He also said he was thankful that he did not kill himself. He talked about how much he enjoyed his family, listening to music, and playing piano concerts.

If you're dead, you can't enjoy this life

Not one person—even you—has lived without enjoying something at some time. Think about when you've been happiest. Maybe it was going to movies, watching television, hanging out with friends, dancing, singing, or enjoying sexual pleasure.

You may get a different perspective if you make a list of the things you have enjoyed. List everything that brought you some fun, satisfaction, or pleasure, even if it doesn't make you feel better right now. The important thing is to recognize aspects of life that make it worth living.

Living In a Stressful World

There is no one cause of teenage suicide. Yet a major factor is the stress that teenagers face. Remember that the rate of suicide committed by teenagers is higher than that of adults. This statistic suggests that there is something especially stressful to teenagers in today's world that young children and adults do not have to cope with.

Being In-Between

Sixteen-year-old Maria was extremely bright and could solve her homework math problems faster than her father could. She cruised the Internet every night, learning about current events and social issues. She had an exceptional vocabulary. She looked like an adult, and she acted like an adult when she baby-sat the neighbor's four children.

Still, Maria, like most sixteen-year-olds, was not an adult. When her older brother teased her, she would complain to her mother. She depended upon her parents to provide her with a place to live, food, and clothes and with an allowance for other expenses. If she was sick, she depended upon her parents to call a doctor or take her to a doctor. When she didn't have plans with her friends on a weekend, she assumed she would do something

5

with her parents, who were her back-up social life. When the television in her room stopped working, she expected her parents to make arrangements to have it fixed.

Teenagers are not children, and they are not adults. They vary individually in their degree of emotional and psychological dependence on their parents or adult guardians. This creates confusion and stress for many teens, because they are never sure how to act.

Gender Identity

Rick, seventeen, didn't like to participate in contact sports, such as football. He preferred to read adventure novels and watch television. He wanted girls to like him and be attracted to him, but he was shy around his female classmates. He envied boys who seemed confident with girls and hoped he would eventually become more comfortable around them.

Being a teen means finding out who you are. A big part of this is learning about gender identity—what it means to be male or female.

There is a lot of pressure to adopt gender roles that society promotes. Teens are brought up to believe, for example, that young men should be tough and athletic, or that young women should be intensely concerned with their body image. Trying to fit into these unrealistic stereotypes can leave teens feeling confused.

Romantic Relationships

Part of a teenager's development from childhood to adulthood is forming a sexually intimate relationship with a partner. You are entering the world of adult sexuality, and this world can be very confusing. As friendships among adolescents become more intimate and lead to physical relationships, teens need to make critical decisions. It can be a stressful time as they develop their sexual identities and progress toward adulthood.

Teens who are gay and lesbian also struggle with certain stresses unique to homosexuals. Sadly, the rate of attempted suicide by gay teens is two to three times higher than that of their heterosexual counterparts.

Peter, seventeen, was brought up in an "all-American" family. His parents encouraged him to go out with girls. They taught him that it was normal to want to get married someday.

Meanwhile, Peter knew he was different from other boys. Since he was twelve he had been fantasizing about other boys and worrying that he might be gay.

As Peter grew older, he learned to avoid all questions about sexuality. He felt uncomfortable when his relatives continually asked if he had a girlfriend. Even worse, girls at school flirted with him. Peter wanted to talk to his dad about his confusions, but he thought his dad would not understand. He was having trouble sleeping and felt pressure to act like someone he wasn't.

7

Many gay or bisexual teenagers realized that they were different from their heterosexual peers when they were very young. Others don't realize it until they are in their teens, or older. However, most people, gay or not, come to realize at some time in their lives society's negative attitude—that being gay is somehow sick or immoral. While this is untrue, it makes life especially difficult for teens who are struggling to find out who they are.

Some teens respond to this pressure by adopting their parents' and society's biases against gay people. They become critical of themselves and think that something is wrong with them. These problems of coping with anti-gay attitudes and hostilities put gay teenagers in a group at risk for suicide. Unfortunately, some gay teens feel that it's better to commit suicide than face who they really are.

If you are a gay person, you can learn to accept your sexual orientation and to cope with those who are biased against you.

Violence and Crime

When Akiko was sixteen, her older sister was attacked and raped. Akiko became increasingly anxious about being raped, especially when she read that women have a one-in-five chance of being assaulted during their lifetimes. About this same time, another student in her school was in the process of legally charging her uncle with statutory rape.

The more Akiko worried about rape, the more

upset she became. She isolated herself from all the men in her life, including her boyfriend, and spent a lot of time locked in her bedroom. She felt that she couldn't trust anyone.

You may be one of the many teenagers who knows someone who was a victim of a violent crime. You yourself may have been a victim of violence or crime.

You have read in the newspapers or watched on television reports of violence in schools, such as students shooting other students or teachers. You may have been threatened with being beaten up on the school grounds and thought of joining a gang for safety.

The world today seems to be a very violent place. From the bombings in Northern Ireland, ethnic cleansing in Bosnia, and terrorist activity in the United States, we have constant reminders of widespread violence in our society. You also know about violent acts of nature, such as floods or hurricanes, that kill people. Life may seem precarious, and thinking about the many ways we can be victims of violence is stressful.

Ethnic and Cultural Differences

As today's communities become more of a cultural, ethnic, and religious mix, teens are interacting with an increasingly diverse group of people. Sometimes, however, differences among people can lead to misunderstandings or even disagreements. In turn, misunderstandings and disagreements can lead to stress.

Having parents with different ethnic, religious, and

cultural backgrounds can be a source of stress and confusion for teens who are trying to find their own identity.

Kaiya, fifteen, was the daughter of an African American father and a Caucasian American mother. She never really thought too much about race, but when she started high school Kaiya suddenly felt self-conscious about her family. Most of her friends were African American, and they often teased Kaiya for acting "white." The more this happened, the more Kaiya felt uncomfortable with her mother. She knew it was wrong to think this way, and she frequently woke up in the middle of the night from bad dreams and stomachaches.

Competition and the Bottom Line

Our culture seems to be obsessed with speed. We want faster machines and better computers. We want microwaves that cook food faster than stoves. The push is on to get through school and climb the ladder of financial success as quickly as possible. Children are urged to "grow up" and act like adults. Teenagers are pressured to decide now what they want to do for the rest of their lives and then to start preparing to do it.

A result of the era of instant accomplishment is that teens have less tolerance for allowing slow, gradual processes to move them toward a goal—and a step-by-step process is needed to accomplish many goals.

Teenagers are pressured to compete and be "a winner," which frequently is measured in our society by grades or

10

dollars. Teenagers who shoot baskets on the corner play-ground are dreaming that they will someday be great bas-ketball players like Michael Jordan and make millions of dollars. And the teens intrigued by cyberspace know about Bill Gates, his fame, and his billions of dollars. Yet not every high school singer and dancer will become a Garth Brooks or a Madonna. Not every adolescent writer will become a Stephen King or a Danielle Steel. Not every would-be scientist will become an Albert Einstein.

The pressure to compete and to be number one is pow-erful. It causes stress because only one person can be on top. Only one student can achieve the best grade in the class, and the struggle to be the "best" is difficult.

Teens see so many rich and famous people on televi-sion, that it's natural to want to be just as rich and famous as the celebrities. Although it is good to try to achieve your dreams, millions of teens will never join the ranks of the rich and famous. This realization can be a blow to their self-esteem.

When John was three years old, his parents got him into the "best" nursery school in town. As he grew older, John's parents put pressure on him to get top grades and encouraged him to succeed as well as his wealthy grandfather. John's father was a successful executive in a large, well-known cor-poration.

John felt that he might never fulfill the expectations of his family. He had always done well in school, but in his senior year his grades began to drop. He discov-ered he would rather hang out with friends in the *evenings than study. The pressure to succeed was beginning to get to him. He said half seriously that he'd like to travel instead of attend college, which shocked his parents. They couldn't understand his lack of interest in school and in achieving. John became depressed and withdrew from his friends.*

Family Issues

Parents Who Fight

About half of all marriages end in divorce. Broken homes are often blamed for the troubles of youth, but the problem actually may be the influence of troubled marriages, regardless of whether the parents stay together or divorce.

Living with parents who are constantly complaining, disagreeing, and fighting—as well as living in a home filled with anxiety and tension—is stressful to teenagers.

Teenagers may feel that they have to take sides in their parents' marital disputes Often, parents use their children as emotional "bargaining chips" and try to win their sympathy. Having to take sides in their parents' arguments is especially hurtful for teens.

When Andy was in seventh grade, his parents began having intense arguments. His father would yell at his mother and storm out of the house. At first his father would just walk around the block and come home, but recently he had begun to go out and not come home for a day or two. Sometimes the family wondered if he would ever return.

During one of their fights, his mother accused his father of having a girlfriend. His father got really angry at his mother and shoved her. Andy put himself between them. He was afraid his father would hit him, but he did it anyway. His father yelled at both of them and left the house for good. Andy's mother cried every night and told Andy what a bad person his father was. Then his father called one day and asked Andy if he wanted to live with him. Andy did want to, but he worried about his mother living all alone.

If parents divorce, it affects teenagers deeply. They may be forced to choose between their parents. They may even be called to testify in court against one parent or the other. Or they may hear a judge declare that one of their parents is unfit.

Physical and Sexual Abuse

Some parents reach their breaking point and begin to physically hit their teenagers. If they spanked their children when they were young, now they slap their faces, or strike them. Although some teenagers cope with being abused by becoming abusers themselves, others turn the abuse against themselves and become self-destructive or suicidal. Incest and other forms of sexual abuse are further examples of ways in which teens' lives can be poorly influenced.

Harriet, fifteen, was in a troubled family. Her father argued and fought with her mother. He had a violent temper and was very mean to her mother. He made Harriet his confidant. He telephoned her from work to ask what mood her mother was in, told her his troubles with her mother, and even described how frustrating their sex life was. Harriet was pleased that her father thought well enough of her to tell her all this, but she also thought she was disloyal to her mother in listening to her father.

Harriet's mother withdrew from the children and began making a life of her own with her friends, going out evenings to school. She became more insistent that Harriet, the oldest daughter, take over more of the household tasks, such as cleaning the house and cooking meals. Harriet became the "little mother" and took charge of the younger children.

Instead of resolving his disagreements with his wife, Harriet's father, who had confided in his daughter, began seeking comfort from her. The first couple of times that her father hugged her in a "too intimate way," she told her mother. But her mother turned it around and criticized her for wearing short skirts and being seductive with her father. She was surprised and even thought that her mother might be jealous of her.

When the younger children were in bed and her mother was at school, her father began holding her in a more sexual way and fondling her breasts. She felt she was left alone to deal with her father. On the other hand, she felt sorry for him. She wanted to please him and make him happy, so she made fewer protests and let him touch her in sexually inappropriate ways. He was gentle and affectionate. She knew it was wrong, but she felt trapped.

Help and Hope

If you feel overwhelmed by pressures such as these, you don't have to bear them in silence.

If you are in an abusive situation or have been a victim of violence, take immediate action. Hotlines are listed at the end of this book that are staffed by caring people who can help you.

Even everyday stress can become harmful when it builds up inside of you. But it is possible to cope. In the following chapter you will learn some ways to do so.

Coping With Stress

A certain amount of stress is inevitable. Basically, you have to cope with stress sometime; you cannot avoid it. But the ways in which you cope with stress can be the difference between your becoming frustrated and unhappy or becoming satisfied and enjoying life.

Destructive ways of coping with stress lead you to be depressed and suicidal. Constructive ways put you on the path to life.

You are better able to cope with stress if you have a variety of constructive ways of coping and are able to adapt them to a specific situation or person. Keys help you to open doors, but every lock takes a different key. If one strategy doesn't work, you can try another.

You may think that you have tried all the possible ways to change the stressful situations that you are in or to change the people you are involved with. But consider the ways suggested here and throughout this book. There is a way you haven't tried yet. Also, even if you are not able to make changes in situations or people at this time, there are still other constructive ways to cope with stress.

No matter what you're feeling, you must remember that suicide is *not* a coping technique.

Speaking Up

John, thirteen, was playing a computer game, and his sister Jody kept telling him which move to make. He yelled to his mother in the next room, "Hey, Mom, Jody is bothering me again." Mom yelled back, "Hey, kids, work it out yourselves—I'm busy." John sighed. It was so unfair; his sister was always bothering him, and his mother was always ignoring both of them. Well, he was sick of it.

John chose to raise his voice. He shouted, "Leave me alone. Get out of here." Mom heard this clearly and came into the room. He told his mother that his sister was bothering him by telling him what moves to make in the computer game. Jody tried to shift the blame by accusing John of not sharing his games, but Mom wasn't buying it. "Leave your brother alone," she told Jody; "it's his game, and he should be able to play it in peace."

John couldn't believe it. Mom was actually taking his side. He felt so grateful, that he even offered to let Jody play the next game.

Luckily, John chose the appropriate coping technique for his situation. If he had insulted, or even hit, his sister, his mother would have been extremely angry. As it turned out, she was sympathetic to his problem and was able to help. The difference is in learning to express your feelings appropriately.

Negotiating

To change stressful situations, you can negotiate to try to get what you want. Negotiation is a way to resolve a disagreement between two people about doing something, such as doing homework now or going to bed at 11 PM.

Stressful situations are frustrating and may be annoying, but to negotiate, you have to suppress your annoyance and take off your boxing gloves. Negotiation is not a fight; it's a process that leads to a good compromise.

For example, in a negotiation a teenager and a parent disagree about what they want to do at a specific time and place. When disagreements are stated, a teenager might say, "I want to go to Julio's house for dinner tonight," and a parent might say, "I don't want you to go to Julio's house for dinner." Some teenagers and some parents think this is the end of a negotiation, but it is really just the beginning.

Negotiation is a back and forth process. Each person presents reasons for his or her position and—what is often neglected—responds to each reason given by the other side. The goal is to persuade the other person to change his or her mind and genuinely agree with you. Then you both have a "win/win" solution. Typically, win/win solutions are the only way for two people in a family both to increase their percentage of "wins."

> *Flora, fourteen, wanted to stay overnight with a friend, Charity. Her mother said that she didn't want her to do this.*
> *Mom: I don't want you going around town late at night. It's too dangerous.*
> *Flora: I'll be all right. We are just going to stay at her house, and her parents will be home.*
> *Mom: I don't know...*
> *Flora: C'mon, Mom. You know I haven't made any*

friends since we've moved. Charity and I have a lot in common.

Mom: Yes, I have wanted you to be more friendly with students at school. So who else is going to be there?

Flora: Just Charity and me.

Mom: This is a school night, and you have home-work to do.

Flora: I'll take my homework with me. We're in the same class and can do it together.

Mom: If you stay up late, you won't be alert at school tomorrow.

Flora: I'll go to bed by midnight, and that will give me seven hours of sleep. Besides, tomorrow is a half day.

Mom: Have you asked her mother?

Flora: She said it was all right. I really want to do this; it would mean a lot to me.

Mom: O.K., you can do it tonight, but I don't want it to become a habit on school nights.

Negotiation is the business part of relationships, but it's no longer negotiation if one or the other person gets angry, puts the other down, calls the other party names, brings up hurts of the past, and so on. If you want to fight or express your anger, don't start negotiating in the first place. At any point in the above negotiation, Flora or her mother could have ruined the negotiation by making a cutting remark, such as "You never let me do anything" or "You always disagree with me; why can't you be happy with what you have? "If this had occurred, neither Flora nor her mother would have been satisfied.

Getting Off the Merry-Go-Round

If you keep trying the same thing over and over and it doesn't work, you are probably on a merry-go-round.

Jamal left his dirty dishes on the breakfast table every morning. So every morning Jamal's father cleaned up the kitchen, and every afternoon he scolded Jamal when the boy came home from school.

Jamal and his dad went through this over and over again. And Jamal's dad was getting mad. A big argument was sure to happen.

Jamal and his father were on a merry-go-round. Jamal was "forgetting" to do his chores because, deep inside, he was frustrated by his family. Jamal's father was avoiding talking to Jamal about it, and pressure was building up.

To get off this merry-go-round, either Jamal or his father—or both of them—can change their ways of coping. Jamal can try something different and clean up after himself, which could stop the merry-go-round. Also, if he is trying to defy his family, he might talk about his frustrations and negotiate what to do. His father can stop the merry-go-round by not doing Jamal's dishes. He can tell Jamal that he is not going to continue cleaning up after him.

It's usually a good idea to discuss your feelings instead of letting negative emotions build up. By talking about situations, you can help to change them, and changing situations will lower your stress.

Coping When You Can't Change a Stressful Situation

On the other hand, you may not be able immediately to change the situations of stress that you are in. But you can find ways to escape them temporarily. If you are stuck in stressful situations for the time being, you can comfort yourself in ways that are available to you at any time.

All of the constructive ways of coping described below help to relieve the effects of stress.

Let Off Steam

If you are a suicidal teenager, you can help yourself by having "escape hatches." An escape hatch is like an opening for the escape of steam in a pressure cooker. It's better to let the steam escape than to let the pressure build until the pot explodes.

You may be in a certain frustrating situation and feel trapped, helpless, and hopeless. Yet the more you stay in the situation, the more the pressure of feeling trapped, helpless, and hopeless builds. You need to let some steam escape to prevent yourself from reaching the point of explosion.

Suicidal teenagers think of suicide as a way of solving their problems. But suicide does not solve problems; it kills teenagers. Having an "escape hatch" is a way of staying alive and still coping with problems. If you are suicidal, something needs to change, and escaping school, work, home, and so on is a way of making a change.

You have many "little" and "big" ways to get away that are constructive:

↝ You can sit and shut your eyes, go to your room, take a walk around the block, go to a movie, or visit neighbors or friends.

↝ You probably can get away from everyone by going into the bathroom and locking the door. Then you have some privacy.

↝ If you like to listen to music, you can use headphones that shut out the sounds of the outside world.

↝ You can go for a walk or a bike ride. You might even go to a school that is out of your area or stay temporarily with relatives or friends who are beyond walking distance from your home.

All people need a "getaway" once in a while from the stress of their activities. A temporary retreat from the world refreshes you. In the face of struggles and problems, a strategic retreat provides a new perspective and may give you a way out of feeling helpless and hopeless.

Comfort Yourself

You may not be able to change some stressful situations or escape them at this time. But you still may cope by comforting yourself. This is a way to make your situation more tolerable until you can do something about it. It's a constructive way of repairing yourself or symbolically "licking your wounds," if you were hurt or damaged by some type of stress. Also, it's another way of restoring your energies.

Feeling Sad and Crying

Regardless of what makes you sad, a natural reaction is to cry. You may help yourself cope with stress and repair the damage of being hurt by feeling sad and crying.

Some teens learned as children not to cry. If they cried, they were called names or teased. Parents may have meant well by punishing them if they cried, by pressuring them to keep "a stiff upper lip," or by urging them to go out and play. As a result, these teens learned to stifle their crying, to paste a smile on their faces, and to wear a mask.

Male teenagers especially may have been taught that it's not manly to cry. But as you learned not to cry, you also can learn *to* cry. It's an essential way to cope with stress and frustration and to repair yourself.

Pampering

Another way to comfort yourself is to surround yourself with experiences that you find pleasant:

- Swim and float. Maybe there's a public pool in your town, or you live near a beach.

- Take a luxurious, warm bath or shower.

- Smell the roses. Give yourself pleasant aromas and perfumes to smell. Or burn incense.

- Surround yourself with beauty. Whatever beauty means to you, surround yourself with it, as much as you can afford. Sunsets and sunrises are free.

- Grow something—a tree, a shrub, a plant, or grass—that is your very own.

23

↪ Get a pet, such as a bird, fish, dog, or cat. Sometimes owning a pet helps you focus on something other than your own problems

Express Yourself in Creative Arts

One way to cope with a situation or person is through creative arts—poetry, sculpture, music, drama, painting, and dancing. These allow you to express your feelings and also to present many aspects of a situation or a person. It is said that a picture is worth a thousand words. Drawing a picture, for example, of a situation may suggest to you a new view of the situation and new options for coping with it.

Beth, fourteen, was a loner, except for one friend at school. The two of them studied together and shared with one another the family frustrations each had.

Beth drew a picture of her family. She drew her father first. Then she drew her older sister, Morgan, to the right of her father. She was "Daddy's favorite." When her mother insisted that Morgan help with the dishes, her father would take Morgan's side and say she had to do her homework.

Beth drew her mother to the left of her father but left a space to draw her younger brother, Arnold, between them. Arnold was the "sickly baby" of the family, who received a lot of Mother's attention when he didn't feel well. Father often complained that she was spoiling him, so he naturally was placed between them.

Beth drew her older brother, John, the first child in

the family, on the other side, the left side, of her mother, who was proud of his achievements at school. He was an "A" student, popular, and on the football team.

Beth sat back as if she had finished the drawing and then realized that she had left herself out. She had told her friend that she didn't feel as if she were really a part of "the family." Looking at the picture, she saw what she already knew, that she was the only child not next to one parent or the other.

As she studied her picture, she thought about her family situation. Her older sister was dating and spending less time at home, so there were openings for Beth to talk to her father if she wanted to. She liked her older brother. He had had some of the same teachers she was having in school, and she decided to ask him about how best to succeed in their classes. Later, she did, and they compared their ways of getting along with each teacher. She herself was not dating, but she decided to talk to her older sister about boys. Her little brother, Arnold, had been a nuisance to her most of the time, but when he wasn't complaining or demanding, he was not bad.

Mother was the most difficult for her to reach. She had learned to cope with her mother by trying to disappear. But then Beth decided to risk talking to her mother about how she disliked being criticized or told to do things.

You don't have to be a skilled or professional artist to do creative arts. If you are embarrassed to be expressive with other people around, you can do creative arts in a room by yourself, and you don't have to share them with anyone. However, sharing your art may help solve some of your problems.

If You Are in an Abusive Situation

Remember, if you seem to be in an impossible situation of physical or sexual abuse, you must take strong action.

Sharon, fourteen, lived with two alcoholic parents who drank before, during, and after dinner and all evening. And when they drank, they argued with each other, and with her if she got involved. They were both very strict and wouldn't let her out of the house. If she didn't come straight home from school, her mother would slap her.

Sharon had chores to do each morning and after school each day. If she didn't do the chores and do them in the "right" way, they scolded her. In the evenings, she had to do homework. Even on weekends, she had to clean the house and help wash the family clothes.

Sharon's father had a temper, and if she talked back when he told her to do something, he would hit her. He did not just swat her back side with the palm of his hand. Several times he threw her on the floor or hit her with his fist. She had bruises, but her father threatened that if she told anyone, he would really beat her.

Sharon didn't tell anyone, partly out of fear and partly out of family loyalty, and she covered her bruises with makeup. But she lived in constant fear of her father. She thought every day about running away from home.

If you are being hurt or abused, you must tell someone you trust, such as a teacher, guidance counselor, coach, or religious leader. If you don't feel comfortable confiding in anyone you know, call one of the organizations listed at the back of this book. Someone is there who can help you.

What Is Depression?

At some time in your life you probably have felt "blue" or "down in the dumps." You may have broken up with someone or lost a big game. Usually, the feeling passes with time. But if the sadness becomes more intense, to the point at which it interferes with your daily life, you may be suffering from the illness of depression.

Depression can be brought on by many things. Crisis and change, or a family history of depression, can contribute to it. No matter what causes it, though, depression has many serious effects on a person. If teenagers become depressed, they may feel so sad, "down," frustrated, angry, and desperate that they may mistakenly think of suicide as a way to end their unhappiness.

It's important to know if you, or a friend, are depressed, and if you are, to do something to stop being depressed. Take a minute and see if you fit into one or more of the following four circumstances:

➭ You do not have feelings or do not express them.

➭ You do not have friends or do not enjoy them.

➭ You do not do things or do not do what you are capable of doing.

28

⮑ You do not believe in anything, and you have no sense of purpose.

If these describe your feelings, you have both the emotional and physical signs of depression.

Emotional Signs of Depression

⮑ Depressed teenagers feel sad, blue, or "down in the dumps." They lose interest in their usual activities, such as hobbies, sports, and music. They feel bored and may complain that life is monotonous.

⮑ They don't enjoy things they used to enjoy. Nothing seems to make them happy or bring them satisfaction. They don't smile or laugh very much. They lack the energy to try anything new.

⮑ They withdraw from friends and family. Talking with people no longer interests them or brings them happiness. Having friends is a burden. Life is drudgery.

⮑ They feel hopeless and despairing. They think that whatever they do is futile. "It's as good as it gets," and it may get worse.

⮑ Their thoughts are slowed. Their minds may go blank. They feel empty. Life is a void and has no purpose or meaning.

⮑ If they had been religious, they stop praying, stop going to services, stop reading the scriptures or other religious literature. They give up on God or lose their faith.

29

➥ They think that no one cares about them; they feel alone in the world and lonely. They may say they feel as if they were in a black hole.

Jada, sixteen, had been a good student, but now she didn't seem to care if she got good grades or not. She wasn't her "cheerful self" anymore. She asked "Why?" to everything her mother asked her to do. She didn't talk to her school friends at lunch time; instead, she took her lunch to a park across the street from school and ate alone. She walked directly home after school instead of hanging out with friends. When she got home, she no longer wanted to practice her flute lessons. When her mother urged her to practice, she played a little but felt it was a chore. Her brother used to tease her, and she would tease him back. Now, when he teased her, she withdrew, felt picked on, and was tearful.

She used to have a lot to say to her family at the dinner table about what happened at school, but not anymore. She didn't speak, unless someone spoke to her first. When school friends telephoned her in the evening, she asked her mother to tell them that she was busy and would call back later, but she never got around to calling them back. Her sister would invite her to go to a movie and then have a bite afterward, but she would say she didn't feel like seeing a movie.

She would thumb through several magazines but find no interesting articles to read. She spent a lot of time in the mornings trying to decide what to wear to school, but once at school, she would think that she was not dressed right. When Sunday came, she did-n't want to go to church and said she wasn't sure she believed in God anymore. Her father urged her to go to church with him, but she put him off by saying that maybe she would go next week.

Jada developed a gloomy outlook on the future. She began feeling rejected by her parents and think-ing that they liked her younger brother best.

Physical Signs of Depression

Teenagers are usually getting more depressed if they develop the "physical signs" of depression.

↪ Depressed teenagers may literally move slowly, walk slowly, and talk slowly. They may not ges-ture as much as they did before. They may gradu-ally get to a point where they just sit and stare.

↪ They decrease their talking. If they are asked ques-tions, they either do not answer or give one-word answers such as "Yeah," "No," or "O.K." They don't explain their answers. They don't ask ques-tions or initiate topics of conversation. If they speak, they speak in short phrases, such as "the boy from the neighborhood," or incomplete sen-tences, such as, "Well, I think" (end of sentence).

↪ They don't sleep well; they have insomnia. They have trouble going to sleep and may stay awake all night. Or, they may wake up in the middle of the night and be unable to go back to sleep.

⇨ They become fatigued quickly if they do physical activities—even walking. They want to stop and rest. Their bodies feel heavy and sluggish. They find that doing daily chores, such as brushing their teeth and dressing, are as hard as climbing mountains.

⇨ They complain that their bodies hurt, ache, and feel bad. They may have physical symptoms and go to the doctor, but the doctor is unable to diagnose a medical condition.

⇨ They are not hungry and may lose weight. In severe instances, their lack of eating may eventually lead to death. Conversely, the only thing some depressed teens seem to want to do is to eat; they may binge and vomit.

⇨ They have a lack of sexual desire. They don't have romantic thoughts and fantasies. Even if they have sex, it is not very pleasurable to them.

⇨ Some depressed teenagers use alcohol and drugs to try to avoid feeling depressed and to energize themselves. The only time they feel good may be when they get high, so they use more and more drugs or alcohol.

Vijay was a senior in high school and an only child. He was extremely sad when his dog died, and he gradually fell into a deeper and deeper depression. He came home from school, stayed in his room, and grudgingly came to the dinner table with his parents but didn't say much. They asked him how he felt and he answered in a flat, hardly audible tone, "I don't know." He didn't eat much and complained that the food didn't taste good, despite his mother's fixing his favorite dish. The next day, he felt too tired to go to basketball practice, and came directly home after school. He didn't go to sleep until 3 AM. He felt wide awake and listened to music on his headphones. Finally, he dozed off. He didn't want to get up in the morning and told his mother that he felt sick and had cramps in his stomach. His mother thought he was coming down with a cold and allowed him to stay home from school.

Vijay began staying awake all night. He sat in his room with a dim night light, flipped the radio dial and didn't find any music he liked, lay on his bed with his clothes on, and stared at the ceiling until morning. He often said he had a cold and stayed home from school. He napped during the day. One afternoon, he started to fix up his room but stopped because he got tired, especially when he needed a ladder to climb to a high book shelf. He got out a textbook to study, but after reading a page, he just stared at the page. A school friend called to see how he was. He said he had a cold and would call back later. Then he turned off his telephone. He wasn't hungry and didn't eat lunch. His mother wanted him to see the doctor. He didn't want to go and said he'd "be O.K." The next day she became insistent. He said, "No, not yet, maybe in a day or two."

A Change in Feelings

As teenagers become more and more depressed, they may not express their feelings. Gradually, as their depression deepens, they become numb to their own feelings.

- ➭ They may feel rejected and hurt. They think no one loves them or cares about them. They have emotional pain. They may sob quietly and be tearful for several hours at a time. They may cry for specific reasons or sometimes cry for no apparent reason.

- ➭ Depressed teenagers may feel guilty and dwell on mistakes they've made long ago. They may feel guilty even for having negative thoughts about someone. They apologize and say, "I'm sorry," repeatedly.

- ➭ They may be irritable and annoyed. They complain about things and people. The food isn't right; it doesn't taste good. Their teachers gave them too much homework. They begin finding fault with their classmates. They became annoyed when people give them suggestions. They are resentful, and as their depression deepens, they may become bitter.

- ➭ Depressed teenagers may be frustrated with themselves, annoyed at themselves, critical of themselves, and put themselves down. They insult and find fault with themselves. They have contempt for themselves and think they are unlovable, lazy, and unworthy. They think they are worse than they are, may disown their positive traits, and may discount their achievements.

Jenine was a junior in high school when she became depressed. She felt sad and was quiet. She would go to her room and sob in her pillow for many nights in a row. She grumbled about everything. The toast was toasted too much and dried out. The bus driver drove so slowly that it took her forever to get to school. She told a girlfriend, "The boys at school are all stupid jerks." She complained to her parents that her teacher didn't explain the lessons and just repeated what the textbook said. She thought one of her friends was too arrogant and told her, "You think you are better than everyone else." But, then she felt guilty for having criticized her.

She began being critical of herself. She began brooding about what a terrible thing she had done. She repeatedly told her friend that she was sorry and asked what she could do to make up for it. She dwelled on how she was not a good person. She became stuck on a math problem and told her brother that she must be stupid. She failed to get a date with a certain student for a school dance. She thought she was ugly and unlovable. She didn't like her hair; she complained that it was never right. She thought she was overweight.

She began comparing herself negatively with other students. It bothered her that she didn't get her menstrual periods until later than most of her classmates.

It was one more thing that proved she was inferior to her friends.

One day when she was alone in the house after school, she scratched her wrist with a razor. Her brother noticed the scratch and pointed it out to her mother. They asked her about it. At first she said it was an accident, but then said she had done it. She had wondered what it would be like to cut her wrists.

A Downward Spiral

As we saw with Vijay, the more depressed you are, the more you create the circumstances that lead to depression—you spiral downward. Depressed teenagers often become suicidal after they have been on this downward spiral.

A few severely depressed teenagers alternate between being depressed and being hyperactive, energetic, excited, and "manic." It can be difficult to identify teens like this as depressed because they often seem so positive and enthusiastic. But their depressive periods are just as serious as those of the teens who don't experience manic states.

If you think you may be depressed, tell someone you trust. Often it is the only way to prevent a downward spiral. Depression is very common, and there are many ways to treat it. One way is learning how to deal with feelings, which you will read about in the next chapter.

Dealing with Feelings

Everyone naturally feels anger, guilt, or shame at one time or another. Having these feelings does not indicate that someone is suicidal. But the circumstances under which they occur, and the ways they are handled, may influence a person to become depressed or suicidal.

Anger

Anger, and how anger is handled, is one of the most important issues for teenagers in regard to their being suicidal.

> When Joe got to high school, he was too nice to everybody. He had learned to say, "Yes, ma'am," and "Yes, sir." If he disagreed with another student, he tensed his face and the pitch of his voice went up a few notes, but he never lost his temper. When other students were pushing him to get into the lunch line, he let himself be pushed aside and waited. It appeared that he never got angry. He stored anger inside himself and was a walking time bomb.

> Bill, sixteen, was angry at his teacher for giving him a C when he thought he deserved a B. But when

he showed the test to his parents, he said, "I guess I should have studied more." Bill thought Carla liked him, but when he asked her to go to a party, she turned him down. He was probably hurt and angry, but he didn't show it.

His brother borrowed his bicycle without asking him, and when Bill went to use it, it was gone. He shrugged it off saying, "Oh well, he's my brother." Bill was tense but always polite and spoke softly to hide his feelings. No one had ever seen him get really angry.

Even if you asked a suicidal teen if he or she were angry, the answer might be no. But their anger is stored inside. They have had typical frustrations during their lives and the stresses of being teenagers, which naturally cause them to have anger or other negative feelings. Both boys and girls may be taught that they shouldn't get angry. Yet by not releasing their anger, it builds up.

Such feelings may appear to go away with time, but they don't go away. They just go underground (or otherwise stay hidden). The neighbors may report after a teen suicide that the boy or girl was "such a nice, quiet teenager who seemed to be so happy."

Suicidal teens may be socially proper, rule-conforming, and achievement-driven. They seem to be nice to everybody. Ironically, if they attempt suicide, they are not being nice to themselves.

If you were taught not to express anger or if you try not to get angry when you are frustrated, you may have learned ineffective ways to deal with your anger, such as:

➭ Sarcasm. You may have learned not to let anyone know that you were angry and found you could be sarcastic and not be punished or evoke retaliation.

➭ Teasing. If you see that the person you're teasing is not laughing with you, it is not humorous and is not a joke that you are playing.

➭ Warming up and icing. Being friendly, and then when the person relaxes, rejecting him or her.

➭ Ambushing. Waiting for people to say or do something so that you can then criticize them.

➭ Attacking something dear to someone. Criticizing a person's child, family, or favorite hobby rather than criticizing the person himself or herself.

➭ Filibustering. Preventing the person you're annoyed at from getting a word in because you keep talking and talking.

You need to learn to allow your whole body to feel the anger. Genuine anger is felt as a rush in your body.

Taking Anger Out on Yourself

"Boomerang" anger is unexpressed anger directed outward at other people that becomes redirected or turned against yourself. It is like throwing a boomerang that goes away from the thrower toward other people and then circles around and comes back at the thrower.

39

Ginger, seventeen, was angry at her ex-boyfriend for dating her classmate. Previously, after going out with him him for several months, she had thought she might be pregnant with his child. She wasn't pregnant, but remembering the whole incident made her even angrier at him. She took out the dress she wore on their last date and cut it to ribbons with scissors. It had been an expensive dress. She took a photo of the two them and smashed it on the floor, breaking the glass. She resented him for dumping her, and for several weeks, she thought of ways to get revenge. Then, one night when she was alone in the house taking a bath, she cut her wrist with a razor. But she stopped the bleeding herself and bandaged her wrist. She told her parents that she got cut by a broken glass in the kitchen.

Sometimes your immediate anger at someone is added to your stored-up, unexpressed anger at other people and results in an emotion that is very intense. The pressure is so great that you feel it has to be expressed somehow or you will explode. You may recognize that your angry feelings are out of proportion to what the other person did or you feel very guilty for your anger. The result is that you harm, damage, injure, or kill yourself "accidentally"—or intentionally.

Jolie, fifteen, was taught that it was wrong to get angry at her brothers and sisters, her parents, her friends, her teachers, and other people in general. But she was inevitably frustrated by people. When her mother told her she couldn't wear a certain dress to school, she was frustrated and angry at her mother but didn't express it. Instead, she "accidentally" bumped into a table and bruised her thigh. When her brother wouldn't let her watch her favorite TV program, she went into the kitchen to help prepare dinner and "accidentally" cut her finger while she was peeling an apple. She started to get angry at her gymnastics coach for letting someone else take her turn, and then sprained her ankle. Just as she was about to win in a Ping-Pong contest, she made some bad shots and lost the contest. She frequently got a grade a point lower than what she was capable of getting. Jolie was late so many times that her friend stopped making dates to meet.

If you are feeling suicidal, remember that you were not born angry at yourself; you had to learn to direct anger that you felt toward other people back toward yourself. Also, you were not born having guilt feelings. You had to learn to feel guilty for doing something you had been taught was "wrong." And you were not born feeling shame for who you are. You had to learn to have shame and think you should not exist.

Constructive Ways to Express Anger

If the ways that you were taught to handle your feelings were destructive, you can still learn to handle your feelings of anger, guilt, and shame constructively.

You need to express an amount of anger at other people that is appropriate for the situation. If you are angry at people who are frustrating you, you may express it verbally or

41

nonverbally. Here are seven ways to express anger con-structively, depending upon the situation, in verbal and nonverbal ways:

1. Say, "No, stop."

2. Tell the other person, "I'm angry."

3. Raise your voice.

4. Call someone names.

5. Speak with an angry sound, such as a growl.

6. Make an angry face such as a frown, or wrinkle your nose, or make an angry gesture such as a fist in the air.

7. Write down exactly what you'd like to do or say to someone who has made you angry.

If you get angry easily and tend to express your anger impulsively, you especially need to give attention to expressing anger physically in ways that are not destruc-tive, and you need to set limits. Here are three rules for expressing anger physically:

1. Don't injure or damage your own body.

2. Don't injure or damage someone else's body.

3. Don't destroy valuable property.

Releasing anger in a physical way allows it to be dis-charged safely through body action. You may choose to express your anger with physical actions toward an inanimate object like a cushion, pillow, bed, or stuffed chair. The object represents whatever made you mad.

Joshua went to a gym and punched a punching bag. He imagined the punching bag was his teacher. He played tennis and imagined he was hitting the tennis ball at his mother, who yelled at him for staying out after midnight. He felt less angry, and his game actually improved for a while.

Some people think that if you express intense anger you have lost control over your emotions. This is a myth. We are always in control of our actions and should always take responsibility for them.

One suicidal teenager, Oscar, said, "If I get angry, I'll kill someone." He had a lot of anger stored up inside, and it felt to him that if he expressed any anger at all, his rage would come out in an uncontrollable rush. Eventually he learned that he didn't have to kill anyone, but he could let out a little anger and then put the lid on it. He could let out the stored-up anger in stages, a little bit each day.

A lifetime of stored-up anger cannot be expressed constructively all at once—but it can be expressed little by little. You may become more assertive, have a chance to change situations, and be less frustrated and stressed.

Learning to express anger may be a gradual process, but it is an effective one.

Guilt and Shame

Guilt is what people feel if they do something that they think they should not do. You may have guilt feelings for having had certain thoughts, such as thinking of stealing a bicycle; for having had certain feelings, such as angry or sexual feelings; or for having taken certain actions, such as hurting someone or stealing.

Jenna, eighteen, had been a virgin until she was seventeen. She had expected that she would be a virgin until she married, although she didn't remember her mother telling her in so many words not to have sex. Her mother talked about the "good" girls and the "bad" girls, and Jenna knew what she meant.

But Jenna's friends were having sex and telling her about it, and she made up her mind that since her friends were having sex, she would also. She accepted a date with a college student. After they saw a movie, she invited him to her house because her parents were out of town for the weekend. They made out for a while, and then had intercourse. She had mixed feelings about having sex in the first place, and afterward she still had guilt feelings about it. The experience was not especially satisfactory; in fact, it was disappointing.

Jenna's inner voice had told her "No," and she felt guilty for not listening to it.

Many teens come to feel shame if they were taught not to be who they are. For example, when Darrell was a child, his mother said, "I wish you were never born, you cause

44

me so much trouble." As a child Darrell took it seriously and thought his mother really meant it. He did not see that it was just an expression of her anger of the moment.

Some teenagers learned to feel shame for what happened to them and how they were treated. If they were victims of violence, they were treated by the perpetrators as if they were worthless. If they were treated as worthless, they learned to treat themselves as they were treated and feel shame. They may feel as if they are worthless, that they should be discarded—and they may discard themselves by killing themselves.

Expressing Guilt and Shame Constructively

A way to help yourself with guilt feelings, when you have not actually harmed someone, is to ask yourself what you think should happen to people who have the thoughts, feelings, or actions you feel guilty about. You may even find a constructive way to punish yourself in order to relieve your guilt.

Sometimes expressing anger at yourself stirs up more anger at yourself. If you are aware that you feel angry, it is better to release it with a helper present than to go home and express it alone in a room.

If you are angry at yourself, you can call yourself names. If you feel guilty, you can punish yourself by making yourself stand on one foot for five minutes. If you are ashamed, you can do what is natural and hide. You can hide behind a chair or under the covers in your room for a certain time to punish yourself. If you have fear or anxiety, a natural response is to run. You can go out and run as fast as you can for fifty yards. You can even run in place.

There is no way to undo who one is, but there are ways to overcome shame. One way is to join movements that honor who you are. In the sixties, "black power" included learning about one's African heritage and taking pride in being an African American. The gay movement also countered shame by calling itself "gay pride." The women's movement supports women for not submitting to men, for developing themselves, and for taking pride in being female.

If you can find a constructive way to express every thought, feeling, and impulse you have, you learn not to judge yourself negatively. In this way, you may come to believe that you energize yourself, are the source of your own happiness, and feel that you are fully in charge of your life.

Friends and Family

Suicide is not just a personal act. Your relationships with individuals—family members, boyfriends, girlfriends, classmates, friends—and with groups of people—peers, families, cliques, cults, and ethnic and cultural groups—may influence you to become suicidal.

You may not be aware of other people's influences on you to be suicidal. By becoming aware of these influences, you take a step toward freeing yourself from their unseen, and often gradual, effects on you. You give yourself a chance to oppose these influences. You may also try to change the ways of thinking of those who are influencing you to be suicidal.

Troubled and Broken Romantic Relationships

Jill, a sophomore, had a boyfriend who was a senior. They had an instant attraction to each other and developed a deep friendship. They spent every free minute together. They couldn't get enough of each other. With statements of undying love and promises, her boyfriend left town to go to college. Six months later, he fell in love with another girl. When he finally stopped writing and then told Jill that he had another girlfriend, she was devastated. She cried, was despondent, and didn't want to eat. Finally, she told a girlfriend that she couldn't live without him and didn't want to live anymore. Her girlfriend persuaded her to talk to the school guidance counselor.

Troubled romantic relationships may influence teenagers to become depressed or suicidal. A romantic couple may become frustrated with each other, or have disagreements and fights.

If a romantic relationship breaks up, teenagers suffer the loss of a friend and loved one. So, after a breakup, teens naturally become sad, "down," and depressed. Even if they initiated the breakup, they still suffer the loss. And if the other partner broke off the relationship, they feel rejected, hurt, and angry. When they become depressed, they may be so unhappy that they think of suicide as a way to end their unhappiness.

If you are a teenager, you may feel as if you need this one person to survive, which sounds romantic, but you do not need anyone to survive now, except yourself. You can rely on yourself to generate your own well-being. If you love yourself enough, you can find ways to satisfy your own needs and wants. It may be hard to accept that a relationship is really over, but your feelings will become easier to handle.

Gay Male and Lesbian Teenage Romances
Gay and lesbian teenagers have to cope with all the stresses of heterosexual teenagers in romantic relationships—plus more. Gay romances have special problems. Gay couples,

more often than not, have the stress of existing in an anti-gay environment. One partner may want to hide his or her orientation and the other not. Their parents may or may not accept them. Sadly, gay teens have two or three times higher rates of attempted suicide than straight teens.

The Group Influence

Your friends and classmates—your peers—may inadvertently influence you to be suicidal.

Peer groups, cults, and other groups influence teenagers to be suicidal. If one or more members of the same group are suicidal, especially if they are group leaders, all the other members may be influenced to join them in self-destructive behavior. We know this happens, and there are many theories about how and why it happens: It's the herd instinct; people are gregarious, and a teenager's need to belong to a group in the first place makes access to self-destructive behavior more likely. Some experts believe the self-destructiveness of a group member is contagious and like an infectious disease, is caught by other group members. Some believe that joining in even harmful behavior helps teens feel as if they belong to the group. Still others think that teenagers imitate or identify with one another's self-destructiveness.

Copy-cat suicides also occur. One group member's suicide or thoughts of suicide influences other group members. In some high schools, one student's suicide has seemed to be copied by other students. In certain cases, even the method or circumstances of the suicide were copied.

Family Influences

Children are born into families, and families are places where children grow. Thus, it may seem contradictory that your family might also influence you to be suicidal. But some families can and do influence teenagers to attempt suicide.

There is no doubt that depression runs in certain families, but it is debatable how much depression is due to genes and heredity and how much is due to the family members' ways of relating to one another. Since suicide is more common in depressed people than in other people, it is no surprise that suicide also runs in families. The statistics show that if one family member committed suicide, other family members are at risk. More than one-third of families in which one family member committed suicide have more than one family member who committed suicide.

One experience that may influence teenagers to be depressed and suicidal is parents' rejection of them, specifically for things over which they have no control—such as for being who they are.

Christine, fifteen, was the only child in her family. Her father did not want a daughter; he wanted a son. She learned from relatives that he had been upset when she was born, and he made no secret of the fact. He treated her like a boy, and while she liked the attention, Christine was hurt that her father really wanted her to be someone she wasn't.

Her mother repeatedly told Christine how much

she suffered in giving birth to her. When her mother was upset with her, she would say, "I wish I had never had you." Christine tried to make up for her mother's suffering by being a "good girl." She ended up putting on a smiling mask and hiding her frustration and anger inside herself. At school, she tried everything to please her teachers, and even though she was a good student, she felt as if she could never do enough to deserve anyone's attention or affection. In her first year of high school, she became depressed and told a school guidance counselor, "I wish I was never born." She said she had had thoughts of committing suicide since she was seven years old.

Generally, parents have great influence over their children. And when parents inappropriately scold, discipline, or criticize their children, they inadvertently tell them not to exist. When parents are frustrated and annoyed by their children, they may say, "Stop bothering me," "Go to hell," "Shut up," "Drop dead," and so on. Teenagers may not realize that this is their anger talking, and that they don't mean it literally. Teenagers may remember these statements from childhood as commands to kill themselves.

Teens may also "use" suicide as a bargaining chip within their troubled family.

Carmen was fifteen. In her family, her parents argued and fought a lot about spending money and about what the children could do or not do. Carmen was a quiet child who stayed to herself much of the time and was depressed. She told her sister that she was so unhappy she was thinking of killing herself. Her sister told her mother and father.

Her parents stopped arguing. The issues about spending money and what the other children could do or not do were discussed privately and calmly. The parents' attention was on Carmen and getting her to talk to their priest. Carmen did, became less depressed, and stopped talking about suicide.

When Carmen felt better, the parents began arguing again. After two weeks, Carmen again told her sister she was depressed and wanted to kill herself. Again, the parents were told and they stopped arguing and focused attention on Carmen.

The repetition of parents' arguments and teenagers' talk of suicide becomes a cycle that escalates. Each time parents go back to arguing, their arguments become worse than before, and each time a teenager talks of killing herself, her talk may be more serious. The cycle may spiral into the parents divorcing and/or the teenager committing suicide.

If you are a teenager, you are not the cause of your parents' fighting. All couples have disagreements, and healthy couples fight sometimes. If couples are troubled, they may fight too much about too many issues and not resolve them by negotiating in a satisfactory manner. If parents didn't have you to fight about—such as how long to let you stay out at night or what friends to let you have—they would be fighting about something else, such as their in-laws or the family budget. You are not the problem in your parents' marriage; your parents are.

Of course, when you come down to it, it is not your family or your parents that cause you to commit suicide, it is you. You are responsible if you take the action of killing yourself and don't explore other options. Parents are only responsible for what they do to you—not for what you do to yourself.

Deaths and Their Influence on Teen Suicide

Loss of Someone Close to You

When teens lose a close friend or loved one, they suffer a loss, may become depressed, and may be so unhappy that they think of ending it all by suicide. In addition, the death of a loved one brings thoughts of death and what it means to be alive or dead. In some teenagers, this sets off a preoccupation with death and dying.

Just as we unconsciously identify with the living, we can also identify with someone who has died. Identifying with the dead is one aspect of natural mourning, and part of mourning is that the mourner becomes like the deceased in some ways without being aware of it.

You may identify with someone who has died without knowing it. By doing so, you may be motivated to imitate him or her. Usually teenagers have liked, loved, admired, and consciously wanted to be like the deceased when they identify with him or her, but they may also have feared and hated the person.

Peter, fifteen, an only son, was close to his mother but feared his father. When he was thirteen,

53

his mother died suddenly. Peter took her loss very hard. He cried for hours. He withdrew into his room, wouldn't talk to anyone, and was moody and irritable.

His father hired a live-in au pair to take care of him. Peter finally returned to school, but he was morose and his grades dropped. He didn't spend any time with his friends.

His mother had been very religious, and Peter had gone with her to church each Sunday. On the second Christmas after she died, he began talking a lot about his mother. He went to Christmas Eve mass and sat in the same pew that she had sat in for years. He insisted that the au pair prepare the same meal on Christmas Day that his mother had made. For the first time since her death, he opened up to his father about how sad he was to have lost his mother. He talked about how he hoped to be reunited with her in heaven when he died. This talk seemed to renew his friendship with his father.

The next day, Peter's father went to work, and the au pair had a holiday. Peter left a note on the table under the crucifix in his room asking God to forgive him for the sin of killing himself and all his other sins. He also described how much he wanted to join his mother and how miserable he had been. He put a picture of his mother on a pillow beside him in bed and held her prayer beads in his hands as he took an overdose of sleeping pills and died.

Peter had not been able to separate emotionally from his mother while she was alive, and after she died he did not overcome his depression. He both wanted to be with his mother and to be like her.

Guilt About a Death

Feelings of guilt about causing the death of a loved one can play a part in influencing teens to be suicidal, even if they did not actually cause the death.

Maura, eighteen, went to a party with her boyfriend. They were dating steadily, had had sex on several occasions, and were serious about getting married someday. They both drank quite a bit at the party. Afterward he wanted to make out, but she was tired and didn't want to. They had an argument, and she became very angry, said she did not want to see him again, and told him to drop dead. He was furious and sped out of her driveway. He was killed in an accident on his way home. The police said he was drunk when his car swerved off the road and hit a tree.

Maura was shocked when she heard the news of his death and was flooded with thoughts and feelings. She felt sad and cried. She felt guilty and blamed herself for fighting with him just before his death. She was angry at him when she told him to drop dead, and felt guilty when he actually was dead. She also blamed herself for his death because she had drunk with him. She felt strange about herself, as well. She thought that she must be cursed and that no man would ever want to be her boyfriend again—she gave men the "kiss of death." She thought she should have been the one who was killed and not him, that she did not deserve to live, and that she should kill herself.

By talking about her guilt, recalling the exact details of his death, and crying over her loss, she eventually overcame her suicidal thinking and didn't try to kill herself.

Maura's guilt over her boyfriend's death was not the first time she had blamed herself for what happened to other people. She had blamed herself for her brother Joey's bicycle accident, her mother's sickness, and her cousin Margie's getting pregnant by a man Maura had introduced to her.

Female Teenagers Who Lost Pregnancies

Seldom recognized is the impact of abortions, miscarriages, stillbirths, and deaths of a newborn on female teens who were pregnant. Pregnant teens identify with the loss of their fetus or newborn, and they may have the impulse to be joined with their loved one in death. If they felt responsible for their baby's death, their feelings of guilt can increase their preoccupation with suicide.

Sylvia, nineteen, had a baby who died of a respiratory disease when he was only one day old. She dwelled on the image of her newborn child's choking to death and could not get it out of her mind. She went to the George Washington Bridge and threw the baby's hospital wristband into the Hudson River. (Later, Sylvia said she had thought about jumping off the bridge herself so she could die as her baby had.) Then she went home and took an overdose of sleeping pills. Her sister came home, found her semiconscious, and took her to the hospital.

Clearly, Sylvia identified with the baby. As she talked about how she had imagined the baby's suffering, she breathed heavily, coughed, and said she had trouble breathing. Since she had thought of jumping off the bridge, her throwing the baby's wristband from the bridge was a substitute for throwing herself into the river.

Deaths of Loved Ones by Suicide

If teens know someone who died by suicide, this markedly increases the influence toward killing themselves. They may identify not only with the deceased but also with the method of suicide.

Martha's mother killed herself with an overdose of sleeping pills on May 5 last year. Her mother had been depressed and often talked with Martha about how difficult it was to live with a man. The two of them discussed her father's impatience, bad temper, and selfishness, but both of them tried to please him. When her mother died Martha tried to be "father's brave girl," and she didn't cry when he was around. But, she missed her mother, who had been her confidant. She had many of the signs of depression. She had trouble sleeping, didn't want to eat, lost weight, and was often late to school. On the anniversary of her mother's death, she attempted to kill herself by taking an overdose of sleeping pills. Her father got her to a hospital in time to have her stomach pumped, and she survived.

Anger at the deceased for dying and leaving the teenager may be combined with identifying with the deceased.

Ernest Hemingway, the famous novelist, killed himself with a shotgun just as his father had. Father and son were both in their sixties when they committed suicide. Recently, Margaux Hemingway, Ernest Hemingway's granddaughter, also took her own life. The tragedy of suicide seems to run in this family.

Jill had many disagreements with her mother and would get very angry, but she never expressed her feelings. She had been taught to respect her mother. When her mother died, she was depressed and unconsciously "became" her mother. She took over the family meal preparation, made the same dinners that her mother had made, prepared them in the same way her mother had done.

Because her mother was no longer alive, Jill had lost her chance finally to express her anger. Her anger at her mother turned into anger at her "mother inside herself" through identification. She went so far as to place a knife at her stomach and thought of stabbing herself. Jill wasn't even aware that stabbing herself in the stomach would really be like attacking her lost mother.

Since identifying with family members and friends who have died, especially those who died by suicide, motivates some suicides, you may help yourself undo the identification by making a list of how you are similar to and different from the deceased.

Mistaken Thinking

If you or someone you know thinks along the ways described in this chapter, you may be on a path leading to suicide. But if you are, all is not lost. Once you recognize destructive thought patterns, you can change them.

Either-Or Thinking

Either-or thinking limits you to only one of two choices. You do not give yourself other options or a third alternative.

> When sixteen-year-old Sharla thought about doing something, she gave herself either-or choices. When she thought of playing Lotto, she told a friend, "Either I win the Lotto this week, or I will quit playing." She told her mother, "Either I am going to play first-chair violin in the orchestra, or I'm going to stop playing in the orchestra." She told a friend, "Either I get an invitation to Lisa's birthday party this weekend, or I'm not going to be her friend anymore."

These instances of Sharla's either-or thinking seem harmless enough, but if she habitually gave herself and other people either-or choices about many things, this way of thinking would indicate she has suicide potential. Her either-or thinking has the power of ultimatums—do it or else.

Sometimes, the either-or thinking of suicidal teenagers is not a choice between a "bad" thing and a "good" thing, but a choice between two things, both of which are undesirable and both of which would make them unhappy.

These kinds of either-or choices are even more indicative of suicide potential. The teenagers, figuratively speaking, paint themselves into a corner. They must either stay in the corner until the paint dries, which they don't want to do, or step on the fresh paint, which ruins the work they just did. Since neither choice is desirable, they trap themselves and feel hopeless.

Either-or thinking is usually illogical thinking. Most decisions teenagers face are not limited to one of two choices, and especially not limited to one of two undesirable choices.

James, a seventh-grade student, thought he was being logical when he said to himself, "Either I have to spend the evening reading this textbook, which I don't want to do, or I will fail the course, which I also don't want to do."

Actually, James was not being logical. He had many other alternatives. For example, he might have reviewed his notes on the teacher's lecture and passed the course. He might have discussed an upcoming exam with other students and passed the course. If he did not get a good grade on the exam, he might have been able to retake it and then have passed the course.

If you are suicidal, you can learn to identify your own either-or thinking and raise a red flag when you give yourself only one of two choices, especially only one of two undesirable choices. There are usually third alternatives. If you recognize that your friends or family members give themselves either-or choices, you may use your own good judgment every time they do so, to suggest a third choice or several alternatives. In this way, you may help them not to be suicidal.

> *Ellen, a high school student, said, "I am not getting along with my boyfriend. Either I am going to start getting along with him, or I am going to quit dating." Her friend responded by suggesting a third alternative, "You might get along better with a different boyfriend next time if you keep dating."*

Being Alive and Being Dead at the Same Time

Suicidal people deny the reality of death by thinking about being alive and dead at the same time. If you are suicidal, you may be thinking, "Suicide will end my miseries and I will be relieved, peaceful, and tranquil and have peace of mind," but these are feelings of living people. Dead people have no feelings.

A belief in life after death is common to many religions. Some teenagers misuse that religious teaching to deny the reality of death and to be confused about being alive and dead at the same time. They begin to blur the distinctions between life and death and blend the two together. Two such teenagers ended up killing themselves: One had had these thoughts for a long time, and the other developed them shortly before killing herself.

George was very religious, and had begun thinking about life after death. For him, it became an obsession. He had asked priests many questions about it. He tried to envision being in hell or being in heaven. When he was annoyed at his parents, he thought he was going to hell. He'd go to confession and report his negative thoughts, but the idea of going to hell stayed in his mind. He imagined his body being tortured and in pain. Once, he intentionally burned himself with a lit cigarette to see what being in hell would feel like. He also dwelled on the idea of being in heaven. He thought he would be doing what he enjoyed in life, and envisioned playing basketball in heaven as he had done the day before. His religious friends also believed in life after death, but they were much less specific about what heaven and hell were like and accepted not knowing exactly.

George's thoughts about life after death persisted through the years, but he stopped talking about them. He became interested in Buddhist teachings about reincarnation. He read about people having "out of body" experiences. He went to a psychic to see if he could contact his dead grandfather. He read the writings of the skeptic philosopher David Hume, who claimed that we don't know if there is a tomorrow or not and that we're just in the habit of waking up the next day. Reading this made him anxious. He wondered if he had already died and was in heaven now, but he became hungry. He wondered if people in heaven ate food.

He began thinking this life was just an illusion. He wondered if he were an extraterrestrial, but he could not convince himself that he was. Sometimes, when he met a stranger, he had the feeling he had known this person before. Sometimes, familiar friends seemed like strangers. He felt sometimes as if he were not real. He didn't have a strong belief about these ideas, but he also couldn't put them out of his mind.

Dreaming intrigued him. For a while, he thought he dreamed things that later happened, but he gave up planning for events in his dreams. At times, he wasn't sure if he had done something or just dreamed about doing it.

George became depressed and attempted suicide. He was hospitalized, and after discharge from the hospital he continued to be preoccupied with the idea of going to heaven. He gave himself a celestial name, "Ontus," and thought this would be his name in a life after death. He wrote a suicide note, planning in detail his own religious funeral service, the hymns to be played, the scriptures to be read, the prayers to be offered, and the priest whom he wanted to lead the service. He expressed the hope that God would forgive him for killing himself and looked forward to being together with friends and family who had died. One day George shot himself to death.

George's view of the next life was that he would be alive and present at his own funeral as if he were one of the mourners. Clearly, he misused his religious beliefs in life after death to condone suicide as a natural if premature death.

Alli, a teenager, and her nineteen-year-old boyfriend Kip first talked about committing suicide by jumping off a mountain on Valentine's Day. Shortly after, Alli started reading an autobiography of an author's near-death experience, and that was when she started writing about suicide. Her father said later, "She felt like she could cross over to the other side, that it would be a simple thing and we all would be together again down the road" (Denver Post, Sept. 21, 1997, p. 19A). Kip shot himself in his home. About a week later Alli went to the mountaintop where she had sat with him and wrote a suicide note: "I can't even explain how majestic it is. Death is not so bad. As I look around here, death and life have become part of each other. Each gives new meaning to the other." Then she jumped off the mountain to her death.

If your friends or family members are using religious beliefs in life after death to deny the reality of death, you might try to help them not to commit suicide by questioning their denial of the reality of death.

Preoccupation with Death and Dying

Death and dying are difficult topics to think about, and most people do not dwell on them. On the other hand, if you are preoccupied with death and dying and spend more time thinking about them than most teenagers, you need to get on a different path.

Bill actually saw someone who had died and who was lying on the floor of a subway station, and he dreamed about it for weeks. He saw on television the replay of a security camera of a store owner being shot to death in a holdup. He imagined himself being shot and wondered what dying would feel like. For him, there was no resolution of these scenes of death; they just stayed around in his mind. He had fantasies and dreams of people being tortured to death and their arms and legs being cut off. If he sat down to relax, he would recall seeing scenes on television of vultures eating a human corpse. He could not get his mind off the idea of death. If he came down with a cold, he was sure he had cancer and was going to die.

Bill's immediate family were all alive and well, so he sometimes wondered himself why he kept thinking about death. He remembered that he had had thoughts about death and been scared even when he was six years old, but these thoughts were increasing as he became more depressed. He had always been a sociable, outgoing person, and continued to be so outwardly, but between times he would withdraw into his room and feel depressed, sad, remorseful, frustrated, and angry. He began psychotherapy, but for the first few months he seemed to be worse. He told someone, for the first time, his thoughts of killing himself. Gradually, he pulled out of his depression and preoccupation with death.

Bill's obsession with death and dying was extreme. He said he didn't want to have these thoughts, but they had a strange fascination for him. The thoughts seemed to pop into his head from nowhere.

And when they did, he became anxious and aware of his heart's beating fast. Bill seemed to be a candidate for a stress disease.

Creative Arts and Themes of Death and Dying

Death and dying are facts of life. People think, talk, and write about these things. If they express themselves in creative arts, they may turn to these themes. Thus, not every child or teenager who draws a picture of a coffin or a corpse is going to commit suicide. But those people who are preoccupied with these themes may be or become suicidal.

The same is true of artists. Their creative work is a way of expressing something about people and life and death—often in ways that most people do not or cannot express themselves. Part of what they express is the unpleasant side of life, such as miseries, suffering, sickness, and death. Their presentations of the themes of death, dying, murder, and suicide portray "the human condition."

Not all artists who present these themes are suicidal. Most artists are no more depressed or suicidal than most other people. It's a myth that one must suffer, be depressed, or feel so desperate that one is at the point of contemplating suicide in order to become a great artist.

On the other hand, some artists who have been pre-occupied with themes of death, dying, suicide, or homicide have reflected in their work their own personal struggles and suicidal tendencies, as well as the human condition. When we hear of the suicide of artists such as Sylvia Plath, whose poems portrayed themes of death, dying, and suicide, we may think that their art drove them to kill themselves. But Plath's expressions of themes of death and suicide may actually have prolonged her life as ways for her to express her frustrations and anger at other people and herself. Still, a preoccupation with such themes among artists who commited suicide indicates that they were troubled and struggling in their attempts to cope with stress. Their preoccupation was an indication that they were on a path to suicide.

Jill's journal revealed that she had been preoccupied with death, dying, suicide, and homicide. She drew pictures that were interspersed with her writings. With black ink, she drew pictures of caskets, skeletons, ghosts, gravestones, and people being shot and hanged. She quoted in her journal lines from Emily Dickinson's poems about death. With red ink, she drew cuts on bodies with the blood running out. When her aunt died, she drew pictures of her aunt in a coffin and wrote beneath them how her aunt's body was decaying in the graveyard. She drew signs in fancy lettering saying, "Death" and "Suicide." She drew pictures of skulls and crossbones. She drew a picture of a woman, put her own name above the picture, and then blacked out most of the picture with a lead pencil.

Jill was preoccupied with death and dying and needed to talk to someone who would not be too repelled by her thoughts. If she had talked with someone, she might have discovered why she had these obsessions and been able to stop thinking about death and dying.

If you are preoccupied with death and dying, you might explore what this means to you. For some teenagers, images of death and dying reflect their murderous rage toward other people or themselves. Most teens are not aware of how angry they were when they first drew the pictures or had the thoughts.

In sum, teenagers' habit of giving themselves and other people either-or choices, having thoughts about being alive and being dead at the same time, and being preoccupied with death and dying, are indicators that they may be on a path to suicide. By being aware of these indications, you may change your ways of thinking and prevent yourself from having a suicidal crisis.

At the Door of Suicide

You are in a suicidal crisis if you are thinking of killing yourself in the next few minutes, hours, or days.

If you plan to kill yourself soon, you need to take immediate action and get help. Don't wait to see if you will feel better, and don't try to "tough it out alone." Go to a hospital emergency room or dial 911 for the police or Emergency Medical Services (EMS). In addition, talk to your parents, a teacher, your religious leader, and or a friend. In the meantime, get a friend or your parents to stay with you or go with you to a hospital or a psychiatrist.

The Wish to Kill Yourself But Not to Die

If you are thinking of killing yourself, you are probably frustrated, angry, and fed up. You may be fed up with your parents, your teachers, your friends, God, and everything else. You may feel, "It's no use. Why try?"

But this is a very different matter from being dead. Being dead is the end of your life. Thinking of killing yourself may mean that you don't like the way you are living, not that you want to be dead. It may mean that you are frustrated and unhappy; that you feel trapped and see no solution to your problems; that you feel your ship is sinking; or that you think no one hears your calls for help. You may feel desperate and think of suicide as a way to solve your problems. All of this means that you don't like the way you are living. So if you are about to kill yourself, you don't have to do it. You can change how you are feeling and change the situations that are frustrating you. You can get through this and overcome your troubles.

Your thoughts of suicide are signals that you are ready to do something to change the unhappy way you are living. Staying alive and making some changes is a way for you to be happy.

Many adults who wanted to kill themselves or attempted suicide when they were teenagers look back and report that they were feeling miserable, no one seemed to understand or help them, and they didn't know what else to do at the time. But now they are very glad to be alive. They feel good and are happy most of the time. This doesn't mean that they have no frustrations and challenges, but they have developed enough ways to cope with stress that they no longer consider suicide as a solution to their problems.

You Have Enjoyed Something

Despite how bad you may feel now or how hopeless your situation is, you have enjoyed something at one time or another. No one's life has been so bad that she or he never had times of feeling good. If you are thinking of killing yourself, you may have difficulty remembering good times, but they did exist. You *have* enjoyed something. You have enjoyed a friend, belonging to a group or a club, being with your family, listening to music, dancing, reading a poem or a novel, watching television, participating in sports, or just playing around. Or you enjoyed doing nothing, sleeping, or eating. Or you enjoyed a pet, a plant, a sound, a sight, a smell, or a touch. If you stay alive, you can enjoy the kinds of things that you enjoyed before—and much more.

Signs of a Suicidal Crisis

These are the indications that someone is at the door of suicide:

Increased Thoughts of Suicide

If you have had occasional thoughts of suicide, an increase in the number or frequency of these thoughts indicates you are moving to the door of suicide or are in a suicidal crisis. You may suddenly become preoccupied with thoughts of death, murder, or suicide. Your thoughts about daily activities may turn to thoughts of death and suicide.

If you can identify what triggers your suicide thoughts, you have taken an important step in preventing self-destructive behavior. For some teenagers, certain specific thoughts or themes trigger their thoughts of suicide. For example, Maurice was sixteen when his mother committed suicide. Now it is impossible for Maurice to think about his mother without having thoughts of suicide.

Bill, a fifteen year-old, didn't like the fact that he was gay and had previously thought of killing himself because of it. He recognized that if he talked about himself or other people being gay, he was likely to have thoughts of suicide, and this allowed him to be more objective about his suicidal thoughts.

More Specific Thoughts of Suicide

Your thoughts of suicide probably change from general thoughts that life is no good and you want to die to more specific thoughts about killing yourself. You may begin giving yourself reasons to justify killing yourself. From thoughts about your troubles and problems, you begin to think you are in a hopeless situation, see no way out, and are trapped. You shift from thoughts that you are being deprived, not loved, and abused by other people to thoughts that you are unlovable, undeserving, and not a worthwhile person. Subtly, your criticisms of others are turning against yourself.

Changes in Moods

One indication that you are at the door of suicide is a change in mood from depression and sadness to joy, happiness, and energy. This change, oddly enough, may trigger your thoughts of suicide and move you to the door of suicide. If you have been depressed, you are more apt to be suicidal when you are coming out of your depression.

A Lack of Energy

As noted, if you have been depressed, you probably withdrew and lost interest in your friends, family, and schoolwork. You probably felt tired and sluggish and did not want to do anything. You did not have much energy. You may not have cared whether you lived or died but were in no mood to do anything about it.

Much Energy in Suicide

Committing suicide is an action, and it takes energy to complete an action. As you come out of your depression, you may become energetic and active. You begin to get involved with people, rather than withdrawing. You are ready to do something about what has been frustrating, annoying, and stressful. You may begin to express your anger at other people or at yourself more intensely. This is a critical time. It is a time when your anger may boomerang against yourself. If you are depressed, you may be able to help yourself stay alive by recognizing that this is an especially difficult and dangerous time for you.

If you have been depressed, another change of mood suggesting you are at risk of suicide is that your sadness and depression deepen, you get on a downward spiral of depression, and you shift from sadness and depression into feelings of hopelessness, helplessness, and despair. When you see no way to solve your problems, no way to stop being depressed, and are at the point of giving up, you are in a suicidal crisis.

Still another change of moods is indicative of a suicidal crisis. If you have been a calm, unemotional, or submissive and compliant teenager and shift into having genuinely strong angry feelings, expressing your anger at people, thinking of killing people, you are in danger of letting the anger boomerang against yourself.

Recent Stressful Situations and Events

There are situations and events that put some teenagers in a suicidal crisis. It depends somewhat on how recently the situations occurred, the degree of frustration and anger they aroused, and the intensity of their stress on you. One such situation is having a boyfriend or girlfriend reject you. If you recently saw someone die, saw a corpse lying on the street, were a victim or the perpetrator of violence, or had a serious auto accident, you may suddenly be in a suicidal crisis. A recent death of a family member or friend, especially if the death was by suicide, should alert you. Even seeing an animal slaughtered or hit by a car in an accident may set off impulses in some teenagers to kill themselves. Similarly, if teenagers have recently read in a newspaper about some famous person's suicide or homicide, it may activate their own wish to commit suicide.

Withdrawing from Contacts with Other People

Recent changes in your social life may also indicate that you are shifting into a suicidal crisis. If you were previously sociable, you may begin withdrawing, staying home alone, not hanging out with other students, turning down invitations, and so on. You may be getting depressed and be moving toward a suicidal crisis.

Shifting from Thoughts to Plans for Suicide

When you have had thoughts of killing yourself, the thoughts may have been abstract, "I hate life. I hate everybody. I hate the world. I might as well kill myself." This is usually a reaction to frustration. If you have talked in abstract terms about killing yourself, it is a different matter if you begin developing specific plans. When this shift occurs and your thoughts of suicide become practical and concrete, you have taken another step toward suicide.

Having Available a Method of Suicide

The statistics on death by suicide indicate that having the method available is a significant factor. If you have thoughts of suicide or a plan to commit suicide and the method is available, you are more apt to attempt it in a moment of frustration or despair. A loaded gun on the wall or in a drawer is an available lethal method. A medicine cabinet containing medications or drugs such as sleeping pills or morphine-like chemicals may mean danger to you. By contrast, the absence of a method delays your carrying out an act of suicide and allows you time to reconsider your actions.

If you've had thoughts of suicide, you may prevent yourself from implementing them by removing lethal objects or substances. Give them to someone to keep for you, so that in a moment of despair you do not kill yourself.

Writing a Suicide Note

Sometimes writing or even thinking about writing a suicide note indicates that teenagers are at the door to suicide. In writing such notes, the writers are thinking about people who will be reading the notes after they are dead. As mentioned earlier, the writers are having a fantasy of being dead and being alive at the same time to observe what happens after they are dead. They are imagining people reading the suicide note, fantasizing who will discover their body, and wondering what people will think about them after they have committed suicide.

> *Dwayne, eighteen, a suicide, had written a note that specified the details of his funeral service: "Please have Father John, from St. Paul's, do my service and ask him to read the 23rd Psalm, `The Lord is My Shepherd.' And, please have the organist play the song that Elton John played for Princess Di's memorial service. Ask everybody not to send flowers but to make a donation to St. Anne's Home for Children so that some good may come from my death. Ask Father John to pick out the hymns; he knew how I have been feeling, but he couldn't stop what has happened." He added, "To my parents: Don't blame yourselves for what has happened to me. It couldn't be helped. You did the best you could. Please give my CDs to Billy. He liked the same music that I liked. Phyllis always wanted my books and magazines, so you might as well give them to her. So, I leave you all with good wishes that your lives will be happier than mine has been. Goodbye."*

Dwayne's suicide note was personal but indicated that he was emotionally distanced from himself. It was as if he were planning a funeral for someone else who had died of natural causes, not a funeral for someone who expected to die by killing himself. Suicidal teenagers' preparations for what they want to happen after they are dead stand out as a strong indicator that they may end up dead.

Teenagers who write suicide notes are very different from older persons writing a will. Older persons are nearer to the age of natural death, and are planning for the care of their children.

Timing of Suicide Thoughts

If you are on a path to suicide, there are certain times that are harder to face than other times. Although suicides may occur throughout the year, according to statistics on teenagers who have killed themselves, you are more likely to be at the door of suicide at certain times of the calendar year. These times include your own birthday or the birthdays of friends and family; anniversaries of the deaths of family and friends, especially anniversaries of deaths by suicide; and anniversaries of special events such as bar mitzvahs, baptisms, and graduations. Calendar times also include holidays such as Christmas, New Year's Day, and Mother's Day.

Buddy, sixteen, was severely depressed. His mother had died two years earlier. He had been close to her and dependent upon her. On the anniversary of his mother's death he had a fantasy that if he killed himself, he would join her and re-establish their loving bond in heaven. Buddy was seriously suicidal, and his friends persuaded him to admit himself to a hospital. He followed his hospitalization with psychotherapy. Even so, on the following anniversary of his mother's death, he again had thoughts of suicide. This time, however, he had gathered around him many friends, family, and helpers to support him through the time of crisis, and the anniversary passed without incident.

Seasons, times of day, and biological clocks may be critical times for your having thoughts of suicide. Day and night cycles may affect you. You become depressed and/or suicidal in the early morning, at dawn; in the early evening, at dusk; or at midnight. Try to be aware of all of these influences and take them into account when you are feeling depressed and hopeless.

The beginning or ending of an activity or a relationship may trigger your thoughts of suicide: the beginning or ending of an intimate relationship, graduating from junior high school or high school and starting high school or college, going away to summer camp or returning from summer camp, becoming pregnant or ending a pregnancy, starting or ending a job, converting from one religion to another, or moving to a new house or a new city.

Again, knowing your specific times of vulnerability helps to prepare you so that you can anticipate thoughts of suicide and find constructive ways to cope with the stress.

A History of a Previous Suicide Attempt

If you have made a previous suicide attempt and are again thinking of killing yourself, you are at the door of suicide because you have a pathway to it in your brain. A river cuts a path in the earth; the water naturally flows down the riverbed, unless something changes. You are like the water in the river. If you are again thinking of killing yourself, the forces of gravity are drawing you to flow down the old riverbed, your previous suicide attempt.

Actions to Take If You Are in a Suicidal Crisis

As mentioned, if you are thinking of killing yourself in the next few minutes, hours, or days, you are in a suicidal crisis and need to go to a hospital or call for emergency medical services or the police.

Getting Help

One part of your mind knows that if you have had thoughts of killing yourself, something is not right. Another part of your mind probably does not want help. But you just have to listen to your better judgment and be willing to go for help—you need it.

It is best to get your family and friends involved. They may go with you to the hospital emergency room or to see a psychiatrist. It will be easier to have some companionship.

If you, a friend, or family member know a psychiatrist affiliated with a hospital, arrange for him or her to meet you at the emergency room. This makes it easier and quicker; having to wait a long time in an emergency room to see a psychiatrist can be frustrating. If you know and like a certain psychiatrist, you may prefer to talk with him or her. If you are under eighteen years of age, your parents need to be present to give permission and make financial arrangements for you to be evaluated by a psychiatrist.

If you are in a suicidal crisis, ironically, you and your friends and family may need to persist in getting help. You know better than anyone if you are at the door of suicide. If you are, you may need to insist being seen or admitted to a hospital. People can change quickly from being severely depressed and suicidal to seeming to be happy. As a result, police or hospital personnel may not think you need to be taken to a hospital or admitted for observation.

The decision that you are in a suicidal crisis needs to be firm so that you are not swayed to change your mind. You have information that the others do not have. If you are still not admitted to a hospital, you should try to have family and friends come and stay with you. You need to persist until the crisis has passed.

After a Suicidal Crisis

If you have been in a suicidal crisis, attempted suicide, or were hospitalized, and have now made a decision not to kill yourself, you are no longer at the door of suicide. Congratulations. You are alive. And now is the time to make enough changes so that you enjoy life, are happy, fulfilled, and satisfied, and get all of yourself on the path to life. Your decision not to kill yourself is a big step.

However, you cannot change everything instantly. It takes time to turn things around. Don't be surprised if the thoughts return. Many people who have been in a suicidal crisis have another wave of suicidal thoughts within ninety days after the first wave. By being prepared, you can keep talking to people or have follow-up visits with those who helped you in the first suicidal crisis.

If you have negative reactions to the people with whom you were involved before, prepare by making contact with some new friends or other people with whom you can talk if you have another wave of suicidal thoughts.

Your friends and family, and perhaps you too, may think of a suicidal crisis as like having had pneumonia—after a few weeks of treatment in a hospital, you would be cured of the pneumonia. But the cure for suicide may take longer. When your friends and family think that the matter is behind you, it may not be. It took a long time for you to become suicidal, and you may not be cured in only one or two weeks.

After a suicidal crisis, you need to make enough changes in your social life, in your school situation, and in your ways of coping with stress that you are thinking of living, want to live, and are on the path to life—whatever that takes. It may require changing schools, or developing a new lifestyle. But whatever it is, major changes have to occur. And the changes have to arise organically out of who you are so that you can sustain the changes and be cured of suicide.

In other words, a sudden change simply for the sake of change may be necessary for now; but you need to move toward changes that are reinforced by what you like and by friends and people around you. It may take a while for you to change all the things that were influencing you to be suicidal. But it can be done.

After a suicide crisis, treatment programs to help you get on the path to life may include psychiatric follow-up consultation and evaluation (with or without medication) and psychotherapy with a professional on the staff of or associated with the hospital where you were. If you were not hospitalized, it still may be helpful for you to sign up with the outpatient psychiatric clinic of a hospital having an emergency psychiatric service. Then, if you have a sudden impulse to kill yourself, you'll have a place to go immediately where you are known.

Getting Help

Before and After a Suicidal Crisis

If you have had thoughts of suicide or have been depressed, you may help yourself by going to therapy.

Individual Psychotherapy

You may not like the idea of seeking help from psychotherapists. Some teens may say, "I am not mentally ill; why should I see a shrink?" Some people see a social stigma about going to psychotherapy, but there is also a social stigma about having a problem and not doing something to solve it. Of course, you could go without letting anyone know, but you may have to tell your parents if you need financial help.

You may be willing to have the psychotherapy, but your parents may not approve. Still, if you can convince your parents of your need for it, they may help you go to therapy. Which is worse? To have a problem and not seek help with it? Or to have a problem and go to a psychotherapist to solve the problem?

Family Therapy

Teenagers, their siblings, and their parents may go to family therapy together. Often depressed and suicidal teens have disagreements with their parents that contribute to their problems. If parents blame a teenager for having a problem, or the teenager blames the parents for it, that doesn't change the situation. If both the parents and the teenager are willing to work together on a problem, family therapy may be helpful. And if parents want to hide the problem from their friends, no one needs to know that the family goes to therapy.

Group Therapy

If you are depressed or suicidal, group therapy is another option. Sharing your thoughts of suicide and your frustrations with people in a small group of six to eight others provides you with many helpers. In groups you learn that other people have troubles and that you are not alone. Group therapy is a chance for you to try out a way of talking to other people and learning how other people see you. It's a place where you can explore ways of expressing yourself. The group therapist guides the group, providing a safe and forgiving place for all the members to learn by experimenting.

Creative Arts Therapies

Creative arts therapies, such as dance therapy, music therapy, poetry therapy, drama therapy and art therapy, provide some special opportunities. These therapies allow you to express something symbolically and reveal what you are feeling. You can hide or reveal as you wish. Through symbols you are likely to express parts of yourself that would not be revealed in your daily life.

Self-Help Groups

Self-help groups are usually for specific situations. If you are or have been addicted to alcohol and/or drugs,

Alcoholics Anonymous or Narcotics Anonymous are self-help groups that may help you. Others are Overeaters Anonymous and Sex Addiction Anonymous. If you are a victim of incest, Incest Survivors may be helpful to you. If you have had psychotic episodes, Recovery, Inc., is another self-help group. There are many kinds of self-help groups, and no fee is required to go to them. You will find many helpful resources listed at the back of this book.

Psychiatric Treatment

If you are in a suicidal crisis, you need to see a psychiatrist and have an evaluation. The psychiatrist may recommend treatment, and together you can discuss your options.

Hospitalization

A psychiatrist may recommend that you be hospitalized. Being in a hospital lets a staff of professionals help you not kill yourself. This itself may lift a burden from you so that you begin to feel better. A hospital staff provides twenty four-hour treatment, so if you feel suicidal at anytime, day or night, staff are present. A momentary impulse to kill yourself may be fatal at home, but not in a hospital. If you are on medication, the staff provide close regulation of your doses. If you've had trouble sleeping, a good night's sleep with medication can make a great difference in how you feel.

The hospital is like a new place to live. It is not exactly the same as a vacation, but you get away for a while from school, home, friends, and so on—whatever people or situations were part of your frustration. Getting away helps

85

you lower the pressure on yourself. Being a patient relieves people of the responsibility for having to study or work. You are dismissed from responsibilities.

Psychiatric Medications

Medications are powerful and can alter your mood. They can completely remove anxiety and can even put you into a deep sleep. Antidepressant medications are one option for you. New antidepressants are more effective, act faster and have less severe side effects than some of the older ones, but it generally takes three or four weeks before they take full effect. Don't be discouraged if they don't change how you feel right away or for a few weeks. If you are at the door of suicide, medications do not substitute for what hospitalization may accomplish immediately.

Choosing Life

There is a life instinct, the will to live and to grow. It's an unseen natural force. Living things don't have to be taught to grow; they just do it. Teenagers too are born with a force for growing and a will to live.

Four Forces for Living

Four major things happen to people who are choosing to live and are on the path of life. These four things influence or motivate them to live. The four forces for living are the four "F's": feeling, friends, functioning, and faith. These things happen automatically to people whose instincts to grow and live have not been interfered with.

If you are depressed or suicidal, concentrating on these four things will help you.

Having Positive, Loving Feelings

Having and expressing positive or loving feelings is important for leading a happy, healthy life. Enjoyment in living is a matter of both releasing pent-up anger and expressing positive feelings. You have a need to express loving feelings for the sake of your own well-being. These feelings are in you somewhere, and you are not complete unless you express them to yourself and to others.

The more you express loving feelings toward yourself and toward others, the more loving feelings you will have. Maybe you were taught the poverty view of love: There are ten apples; if you give away five apples, you have only five left for yourself. You need to believe in the abundance view of love—that the more apples you give yourself to eat, the more apples you will have to eat, and the more apples you give to other people, the more apples you will have to give to other people.

In loving yourself, you may enjoy the pleasures that are not destructive toward yourself or others, even such basic pleasures as sleeping, eating, and enjoying sensual feelings. You may take an inventory of what you enjoy and give yourself permission to do what you enjoy and explore new ways to enjoy yourself.

Living in the Moment

Feelings are transient and momentary. As mentioned previously, one reason not to kill yourself is that your feelings will change. If your situation seems to be hopeless, if you feel helpless and trapped, and if you are thinking of killing yourself, these thoughts and feelings are occurring in a moment of time. If you feel bad this moment, it may seem as if you have always felt depressed and suicidal. But you have had other moments, and you will have future moments, if you stay alive. You don't have to feel this way forever.

Feelings are not like money. You can save money in the

bank to spend it tomorrow, but you cannot save up good feelings in order to feel good tomorrow. You can enjoy all the good moments that you have today and not worry about tomorrow. You will still have the same number of moments tomorrow.

You can be "rich" or "poor" in happiness only in how you live in moments. The secret of changing is to have more moments that are fulfilling and happy and fewer moments that are miserable.

Friends

One of the things that make your life enjoyable is having friends. But you won't enjoy your friends if you don't express yourself with them. On the other hand, if you express all the anger that you've stored up from the past, they will pull away.

Casey had always had many acquaintances and seemed popular at school, yet he didn't enjoy being with people. When he was with classmates, his mind was on what was the right thing to say. He was polite. He thought he should act a certain way around people, but that was not the way he genuinely felt. He took the same girl to the school parties and dances, so he appeared to have a girlfriend, but he didn't talk with her about what he thought and felt. Their conversations were mostly about school activities. He usually hid what he really felt and rarely spoke all of his thoughts.

The rewards for all this effort were no longer paying

off and were not enough to make him happy. Casey became depressed. He had always done what he was "supposed to do," until lately. He no longer kept up the front of being polite and friendly. His classmates and even his "girlfriend" were beginning to pull away from him. He became more and more depressed. He didn't care if he did his homework, or practiced soccer, and he just didn't feel like cleaning up his room every day.

Casey felt lousy. His teacher criticized him for not completing his homework, and he thought she didn't like him anymore. His mother got on him for not cleaning up his room. His girlfriend turned down his request for a date and seemed to be avoiding him at school. On Saturday mornings, Casey stayed in his room and didn't feel like talking to anyone.

Things got worse. His mother tried to cheer him up and encouraged him to go to parties, but he didn't feel like it. His father urged him to study, and he made a half-hearted effort. He stayed in his room and wondered if life was worthwhile. He began having thoughts of suicide. Finally, his parents confronted him with how he had changed, and he told them that he didn't want to live anymore. They went with him to a psychotherapist, who recommended seeing him for individual sessions and seeing the family for family sessions.

Casey seemed to be friendly enough, but he didn't truly enjoy people. His depression was telling him he needed to change. It was time for Casey to take off his mask and take the risk of letting people know who he *really was. As he began to enjoy his friends, his thoughts of killing himself vanished.*

Nobody can guarantee that you'll make friends if you start telling people what you think or doing what you want to do. What's certain is that things will change. If some people don't like what you say, it gives you an opportunity to argue with them or express some of your negative feelings to them. But you also need people who disagree with you because they help you clarify your own thinking. It's also likely that some different kinds of people will be interested in you.

A network of connections is helpful, even if teenagers disagree, argue, or fight with some people. We usually think of friends as people with whom we relax, but we also need people with whom we do not get along well. Negative interactions are still interactions, and for suicidal teenagers it may be better to have some negative interactions than to have none at all, especially if they can stand their ground and argue back. Some teenagers report that they have arguments and fights every time they visit their cousins, for example. A paraphrase of the old proverb might be, "Keep your old opponents and get new ones."

One Friend Is Not Enough

Some teenagers have only one peer-friend with whom they are close. Having one friend may help, but it is still a form of isolation, quite different from going out and having several friends. You need groups, cliques, and circles of friends of all kinds.

Handling Shyness and Embarrassment

If you are shy or anxious, you probably haven't enjoyed being around people. Your shyness may have helped you cope, survive, and get along. You needed it then, but you don't now. If you talk despite feeling shy, more than half of the people listening to you will hear what you say.

Start with Being Your Own Best Friend

At this moment, you may feel lonely and as if you have no friends. You may be the only person in your room right now. As I said before, if being alone means "being lonely," change your way of looking at it. You are not alone; you are "with yourself." If you have "no friends," that means that you are not your own friend. You don't like the company of yourself.

It's time to love yourself. You are a human being like everyone else, for better or for worse. You weren't born disliking yourself; you had to learn to dislike yourself and your own company. If you are depressed or suicidal, you are probably harder on yourself than on anyone around you. You are probably more critical of yourself than you are of anyone else. You are your own worst enemy.

It's time to change and lighten up on yourself. You need to throw away the old measuring stick and get a new one, get a new sense of values. It's time to let yourself have feelings and do things. You may still like to be with other people, but you can learn to enjoy yourself and not suffer when you are alone. If you are going to make changes, begin by being your own best friend. If you like being with yourself, other people will start liking to be with you.

92

A Plan for Six Friends

If you feel all alone and think that no one loves you, the idea of six friends sounds far out. Let me lay out the plan so that when opportunities come along, you will be ready to identify them and respond. If you genuinely love yourself, you won't have to work at finding friends. You will expose yourself to people, be relaxed and enjoy yourself, and people will come to you naturally.

Think about finding six types of friends. They may be family members but, preferably, are in addition to family members: two older friends, two younger friends, and two friends of your own age.

You learn to receive help, attention, and concern from older friends. Of course, friendships are mutual and you may also give help, attention, and concern. It's not a question of your needing help, although you may, but you learn to receive it graciously. These friends are like father-figures and mother-figures. They may be teachers, other professionals, business people, or community leaders who are interested in you.

You learn to give help, attention, and concern by having two younger friends. You are like a big brother or big sister to friends who are younger than you and toward whom you are caring and protective. They may be students in lower grades or neighbors. If you help younger kids part of the time, you will probably do more in the long run to help yourself.

You learn mutuality with two friends your own age, mutually sharing attention, concerns, interests, values, and goals. They may be classmates with whom you study or play. The opposite-sex friend your own age may be one whom you date but doesn't have to be.

93

The six include three same-sex friends and three opposite-sex friends. Same-sex friends help you understand yourself as a male or female and help you develop your masculine or feminine traits. Opposite-sex friends give you an understanding of how the other half of the world lives and sees things. If you're heterosexual, this may be an important lesson, since a lot of your satisfaction is going to depend on how you get along with an opposite-sex intimate partner.

Where are you going to find six friends, especially if you think you have no friends? First, go where people are. You don't find friends in your own room. Make a list of all the people you know in each of the six categories. Pick one from each list, and give him or her a telephone call, "just to say hello." Tell the person what you have been doing and ask what he or she is doing. If the person is willing to talk or listen, continue the call. If you are not interested, say good-bye—or risk saying that you don't find him or her interesting. At least, you won't be forgotten!

Functioning at Your Best

Another force for living is satisfaction in doing things. You have capacities to do many things. But if you are depressed and suicidal, you may not feel like doing anything. You may not have fun doing things, may feel like a failure, or may feel guilty for not having accomplished more.

Doing Nothing

It's time to make a change and take some risks doing what you want to do. If you are depressed, you may not know what you want to do and may feel like doing nothing. For you, this may be the biggest risk of all—to do nothing. If you feel like doing nothing, experiment with consciously and intentionally doing nothing. Plan to do nothing so that no one interrupts you. Tell your family that you do not want to be disturbed, or hang a sign on your door. Turn off the ringer on your telephone and let the answering machine answer it.

To make "doing nothing" work, you have to honor everything you do and not discount it as worthless, irrelevant, or meaningless. Even when you say you're doing nothing, you must realize that it's absolutely impossible actually to do nothing. By recognizing the things you are doing, you eventually begin to do more things. I know this sounds foolish to some people. They have a "weights and measure" approach to themselves. The only "something" they acknowledge and value is what fits their prior criteria—memorize a page in the textbook, get an A, win a tennis match, go to college. If you matter to yourself, everything you do matters, even scratching an itch.

If you fight against your wish to do nothing, the fight can go on a long time. If you accept doing nothing, eventually doing something will come to mind.

When Debra, eighteen, did nothing, she picked up a pencil and began doodling. Her doodles became faces. Her faces became very artistic pictures. When she had the thought that she should become a famous artist, she lost it. It was no longer fun. When Jonathan did nothing, he eventually began tinkering with his alarm clock. He took it apart and enjoyed doing it. He might never take another clock apart. He had to be free to choose never to do it again, but the idea intrigued him. Fixing clocks became his hobby.

Take Part in the Economy

The other side of doing nothing is doing something that society values and compensates. High school graduates frequently feel they cannot support themselves, especially if they make a minimum wage. Parents may give small children an allowance, but that is not the same as being paid by strangers for doing something. At eight years of age, a child can collect plastic bottles and soda cans and turn them in for cash. If you have money to invest, you can make money investing in something.

Doing something that makes money gives you a niche in the global economy. Spending some time each week making money gives you a start. It helps you feel independent. Spend a little of the money you make for whatever you want to buy. It doesn't matter what you do, and it doesn't mean you have to be self-supporting or let making money interfere with your schooling. Doing something that makes money gives you an anchor. You have something that you can always fall back on if you need to.

Having Faith in Something and a Sense of Purpose

Faith, beliefs, and values are forces for living. Faith or the spiritual quest is to answer the questions: Who am I? Why am I alive? What is the meaning of life and death?

The question, Who am I? may be answered on four levels: who you are mentally, physically, emotionally, and spiritually. As a total person, you are a mind, body, heart, and spirit.

Part of the answer to the question, "Who am I?" is that you are a unique person. Nobody is, has ever been, or ever will be just like you.

Why are you alive? To learn to listen to yourself and hear about your own uniqueness. To learn to thrive and have love and joy.

Personal Belief

Having faith or belief in something is your own personal faith or belief. It may or may not coincide with an established religion. It may or may not be a so-called divine revelation to you or to someone else.

I happen to believe in God. You don't have to believe in my God, but I urge you to have a faith and belief in something that is a positive world view and that gives you a meaning and purpose in your life. This purpose may be revealed to you through believing that who you are is what you were supposed to be. A philosopher, René Descartes, said, "I think, therefore I am." If you think, then you might say your purpose is to think.

A larger plan and a positive world view is a belief that your life matters and is valuable. It begins with being valuable to yourself—you valuing and possessing your life. Whatever you do, you do because "This is your life." Your life is important to you, and every moment is your moment. This is your ship and you are steering it.

If you truly value yourself, you will also value other people. Then your concern for the well-being of other people is automatic. No one has to lay a guilt trip on you to "love your neighbor." If you love yourself, you will "Love your neighbor as you love yourself." Your ways of fulfilling yourself become harmoniously interwoven with the well-being of other people on planet earth.

Although it sounds simple, your positive, life-affirming world view needs to be genuine. Your forces for living need to be realistic and not a recital of platitudes, "Yes, everything will be all right." Instead, you must be aware of your own specific forces to live.

If your positive world view is genuine, it helps you to make realistic assessments of friends and family members. You see and appreciate their positive traits and tolerate their negative traits, as long as they do not abuse you. If your positive world view is genuine, it helps you to understand the despair and hopelessness of friends and family, to see the miseries that some humans suffer, and still not be drawn into their downward spiral. A positive world view and a sense of generating your own well-being means that you will not easily be upset by other people's criticisms or rejections.

One way to help yourself, if you are suicidal, is to review in your mind or make a list of the friends, functions, feelings, and faith that have been part of your life. If you write them down, paste the list on your mirror to remind yourself of them every day, and as a new one happens to you, add it to your list.

Conclusion

Even if you do not fulfill yourself in body (function), in mind (talk with friends), heart (express feelings), or spirit (have faith), there are still many reasons not to kill yourself. Your life *is* worth living.

When Someone You Love Has Committed Suicide

If someone whom you loved has died, this is a loss that you must cope with. If the person died by committing suicide, it is an especially tragic loss because it shouldn't have happened and is a waste of a life that might have been changed.

If the person who committed suicide was a teenager, this was a very premature death. Because suicide stirs so many strong feelings in people and because of the social stigma and shame associated with it, dealing with a loved one's suicide is extremely difficult. If the teenager who committed suicide had a terminal illness, coping with the death is even more complicated.

Although the main focus of this chapter is on friends and family of teenagers who committed suicide, if you are a teenager and your parent has committed suicide this book can help.

If you are the parent, child, family member, or close friend of someone who committed suicide, you are a survivor. The loss of a loved one through suicide is especially stressful and traumatic because it is an unnatural and intentional death.

When people hear that someone has died, one of the first questions they ask is how did the person die. If friends and family answer that he or she died from a heart attack or cancer, people generally say that they are sorry and offer sympathy. If they answer that the person killed himself or herself, people often have a very different reaction. They may be shocked or startled. They may doubt the truth. Or they may react as if they had heard a secret that they were not supposed to know. Puzzlement crosses their faces.

Stages of the Process of Grieving

Friends, family, and other helpers of survivors of teen suicide can be most helpful if they recognize that the survivors need to go through each stage of a difficult grieving process. The stages are: shock, denial, sadness and depression, identification with the dead teenager, guilt, shame, anger, and adjustment. What helpers say and do at each stage helps survivors complete the stage and go on to the next so that they can finish the grieving process and be able to put their lives back together and truly survive. The order of the stages may vary, and the stages may overlap.

Shock

When survivors first hear of the death of a loved one, their initial reaction to the news is shock. They are stunned.

Marcella, the single parent of a teenage son who committed suicide, was shocked to hear the news. Her son had gone to school in the morning as he did every day. Two of her friends happened to be at her house when the police came to her door. They told her that her son was dead and apparently had shot himself. She cried out, "No, no, it can't be." "Oh my

101

God, Oh my God." She clutched and hugged her friends. She recovered momentarily and asked, "Is it true?" "How do you know?" "When did it happen?" "How did it happen?" Each time she heard an answer, it was as if she were struck a blow that stunned her for a moment, and then she asked for more information. Then the police asked her a few questions. They jotted down some facts and figures and said that someone from the department would return later.

She shut the door after the police left, stood staring at the door for what seemed like a long time. One of her friends spoke, and Mary turned around, cried, and said repeatedly, "How could this happen?" "How could this happen?" She hugged her friends again. Then she suddenly stopped crying and asked in a matter of fact way what her friends were preparing for dinner tonight. They didn't know what to say. Then, as if she had just realized her son had died, Mary said, "I have to telephone my sister." She paused. "What should I tell her?" One of her friends answered, "You'd better tell her what happened." Mary agreed and picked up the telephone.

After hearing about a death by suicide, some survivors faint. In a state of shock, some survivors are overwhelmed, confused, numb, and paralyzed and cannot react immediately. When they hear about the death, they may act as if they had been told that the sun was shining. It takes a while for the news to sink in. Some survivors are in a state of disbelief. Some stare into space. Some scream or cry. When shock occurs, a few seconds may seem like an eternity; it's as if time stood still. Or the minds of the survivors may begin to race, and many thoughts and images rapidly pass through their minds.

When people bring the news of a teenager's suicide to the family, they may try to break it gently by saying, "Something has happened; there has been an accident; your child is sick. I think you should come over right away." But, when survivors hear that the teenager is dead, there's not much people can do except to listen, be with them, and wait patiently for them to come out of shock and begin talking.

Denial

As survivors come out of the state of shock and begin to realize what has happened, they may begin the stage of denial. Denial is a time during which survivors continue what Marcella did. They alternate between recognizing what happened and pushing the news out of their minds. After the shock, survivors go back and forth in their minds thinking about the suicide and acting as if they hadn't been told about it for the next several days or more as they attempt to absorb the news.

Denial helps survivors cope. The news may be too much for them to absorb and react to all at once. They "take in" some of it and then "put it out of their minds" for a while. They may wash the dishes or read the newspaper as if they had forgotten about the death, and then suddenly they remember or it "hits them" that someone has died.

A day after hearing that his son had shot himself, one father thought about the time of a television broadcast of a certain basketball game, and then it dawned on him that he had planned to watch it with his son. It seemed as if he had forgotten for a moment about the death. Actually, he had not yet fully received the news. The idea of his son's suicide was too much for him to take in and react to all at once.

During the initial phase of denial, friends, family and other helpers may let the survivors set the pace and wait for them to talk about the teenager who died. Survivors may be stressed if they are reminded too often about the death and are not given time to absorb the news. On the other hand, if survivors do not begin to talk about the death for too long, helpers may eventually initiate talking about it by asking about the funeral arrangements or making comments about the deceased. Survivors know they have to face the death, and if friends and family talk about it, they may feel they are not alone in grieving. Individuals are unique, and there is no precise rule about how to be helpful to each survivor and to know her or his readiness to talk about the death or the deceased.

When the news of the loss is beginning to be received, survivors begin to think about what they will tell other people about the death, whom they will tell, and when they will tell them. As they gradually absorb the fact themselves, they decide what to tell others. A father said, "I don't think we should tell Uncle Bob that Julie committed suicide." Her mother said, "Well, he was close to her, and Julie would want him to know. I think we should tell him." The parents discussed it and finally decided to tell him.

If helpers recognize the importance of the stage of denial, they are careful not to remind survivors of what happened until they are ready to face it. Helpers may judge survivors' readiness to hear the facts by how they prepare to answer people's questions about the death and how it happened.

During the stage of shock or denial, the police may be involved. At a time like this, it seems traumatic to have to have a police investigation, but it is necessary to determine that the cause of death was suicide and not something else, such as homicide. This practical necessity may force survivors to acknowledge the suicide, but if it is too stressful, it may delay or prolong their grieving process. On the other hand, if the death is ruled a suicide by the police, it may help some survivors accept it. Uncertainty about the cause of death may be a stumbling block to survivors resolving the loss of a teenager by suicide, and it may hinder them in getting past the stage of denial.

Sadness and Depression

Survivors have lost someone and are sad about the loss, even if they had many arguments with the deceased or disliked some aspects of him or her. If you are a survivor, you need to let yourself feel sad and cry. One father told me how he did not cry when his son committed suicide. He dealt with the details of the arrangements and comforted his wife, but after two weeks he went alone to a room one night and "bawled his eyes out."

People naturally feel depressed after the loss of someone close. Depression (as described in Chapter 3) is a healthy way of coping with a loss. Survivors may lose their appetite, and may not sleep well. They may not want to do anything, but just sit and stare. If you are a survivor, you may need a vacation from work or other responsibilities to let yourself feel the depression and begin recovering from the loss.

Sadness moves into reminiscing. Reviewing the life of the lost one needs to happen. One parent talked about how her son, who committed suicide at age eighteen, used to eat his oatmeal in the highchair as a baby. Reminiscing is the process of "hanging onto" and "letting go" of the lost one. Survivors do not need to review every detail in the life of the deceased, but review enough to allow healing to occur. Reminiscing triggers the sadness and is also a relief to mourners. Memorial services help the reminiscing. Friends and other helpers need to visit survivors three, six, and ten weeks after the death and listen to or initiate the reminiscences. The time between these moments gradually becomes longer as the grieving process continues.

The Jewish ritual of placing a veil on the tombstone for a year and then removing it seems to capture and institutionalize the mourning process. People who have lost someone dream about the person for nine months—more or less. It may take nine months of having periods of reminiscence to complete the stage of sadness. Going through all the stages is necessary, and some people cling to the reminiscing too long, using it to avoid the later stages, such as guilt and anger.

Identification with the Dead Person

Another stage in coping with the loss of someone close is the psychological process known as identification. Survivors are not usually aware of identifying with the deceased. It happens automatically, and it is a powerful psychological force. It is one of Sigmund Freud's observations that has stood the test of time.

In identifying with the deceased, survivors take on his or her characteristics. It's as if they put on the coat of the dead person and begin to talk and act as he or she talked and acted. They may use the same words that the deceased used, dress the way he or she did, have similar opinions and impulses.

Helpers need to be alert to this identification with the deceased. Through identification, survivors may acquire an impulse to kill themselves. Helpers need to assess that potential and help them to avoid it. Identification with the person who committed suicide is one explanation of the statistic that more than one-third of families in which one member commits suicide will end up having another member die the same way.

On the other hand, the influence on some survivors is just the opposite. The suicide galvanizes some survivors into determination not to kill themselves.

Shame

Survivors of teen suicide have feelings of shame. It is another stage of the grieving process. We live in social groups that have certain attitudes or biases about suicide. There is a social stigma about it. Having a family member commit suicide is like having a family member commit a crime or become psychotic or have a nervous breakdown. These things become family secrets. Survivors generally do not want people to know about them.

Survivors have various reasons not to tell everyone the

whole story of what happened. In the first place, they may not know the whole story. Secondly, some survivors do not want to upset their friends by telling them everything right away. And some survivors are ashamed of the suicide. It may be unclear whether they are ashamed or are still in the denial stage and are not ready themselves to face the facts. They may react by telling only one or two close friends or family members that the teenager took her or his own life. If asked how the teenager died, some survivors cope by saying that he or she died suddenly—and they say it in such a way as to avoid further questions. Some survivors make up a story about what happened. They may tell people that the teenager had an accident, or was sick and died suddenly. They may make up a story that is half true and tell it as if they believed it themselves.

One teenager who committed suicide liked to go hunting. His parents told friends that their son was hunting in the woods and was killed accidentally. Perhaps they half believed it was an accident, because it was too painful or shameful to admit that their son intentionally killed himself.

In order for survivors of teen suicide to overcome shame, they may need to acknowledge their own biases against the families of those who commit suicide. For example, there is also a social stigma about being gay. The shame of being gay is part of the pressure that contributes to the number of gay teenagers who kill themselves. Parents of a gay teenager who committed suicide have to cope with both social biases—against being gay and against suicide.

Guilt

Survivors of a teen suicide may think that they caused the suicide or could have prevented it. "Why didn't I telephone him this morning?" "I should not have upset her last night by telling her to do her homework." "I should have spent more time with my family and not have worked so many evenings."

Survivors try to make sense of what happened and cope with the death by thinking about who, or what, is to blame for the suicide. They may blame themselves and feel guilty. They may blame other people, or the teenager himself. Sometimes they alternate between blaming themselves and other people.

If a death was caused by homicide, survivors blame the murderer, and are intent on his being punished. In the instance of suicide—especially teenage suicide—survivors may also look to place blame. They will show the same amount of anger at whomever they think "caused" the suicide. This can be frustrating, because in the case of suicide, no one is to blame.

As a result, in this void of not knowing why a teen committed suicide, the survivors tend to blame themselves. They may feel that their love was imperfect, as if they should have been unconditionally loving and not have been frustrated or made any demands on him or her. As survivors ponder the events leading to the teenager's suicide, they may keep thinking of something new that they did (or failed to do) that might have prevented it. In long-term relationships such as those between family members and close friends, there is always something more one might have done to be more loving.

When survivors initially blame themselves for a suicide, many helpers try to reassure them that they did not cause it. You may want to reassure them, but it's probably a better plan of action just to listen. Reassurance that it was not their fault may actually lead them to ignore guilty feelings. Sometimes survivors' guilt is irrational and extreme. If a teenager committed suicide, family members may remember long-ago offenses or slights and feel guilty about them. For example, a sister felt guilty for having stolen her dead teenage brother's pencil when she was four years old and he was six. Realistically, this is unlikely to have had any influence on the teenager's suicide.

Self-blame is difficult when any loved one dies, because the person is not around for one to make amends. Self-blame is especially difficult when a loved one commits suicide because people who kill themselves often do it in reaction to their situations and other people. The dead person's reaction to society explicitly or implicitly blames other people.

Still, loved ones need to confess to helpers what they think they did or failed to do that contributed to the suicide. Those who help survivors need to listen to their confessions to help them overcome their guilt. Eventually, survivors need to accept the fact that the teenager chose to kill himself and is responsible for the suicide.

Even if you think that you contributed to the suicide, it's not your fault. Let's say you broke up with your boyfriend who then killed himself. The way you broke up may have contributed to his depression or anger, but you are not responsible for his suicide. He undoubtedly had other influences that led to his suicide, some of which occurred even before he met you. Besides, he had to make the decision to take the final action that killed him. He chose to kill himself, and he chose to do it by whatever method he used.

Anger

In the instance of suicide, the question of blame alternates between survivors blaming themselves, blaming other people, and blaming the dead teenager. And with blame comes anger. Thus, the stage of guilt may overlap the stage of anger.

If a professional, such as a teacher, guidance counselor, physician, clergyperson, or therapist, was involved with the teenager, he or she may be blamed by the survivors. If drugs were involved, the drug sellers may be blamed, and survivors will be angry at them. If the teenager had a close friend, the survivors may blame him or her and be angry, even though the friend is also in mourning.

If you are helping survivors, listen to their blame and their anger. You may be most helpful by letting them blame someone and not trying to be too rational in sorting out immediately who or what was to blame. If survivors have an impulse to take hostile action toward those they blame, helpers may attempt to delay their taking action until they know all the facts.

This stage is very difficult for some survivors, especially when they blame the teenager. Loved ones are not supposed to be critical of the dead. Parents may think that they should not be angry at a teenager who committed suicide. Also, teenagers are never supposed to be angry at parents and especially not when a parent commits suicide. But expressing anger at the deceased is one stage of the grieving process. If survivors cover over or hide their anger, they prolong their sadness and grief.

The dead teenager took an action that resulted in her or his death. In suicide, the responsibility for the act of death lives with the deceased. The teenager made a choice to kill himself or herself or to be in a situation of risk that resulted in death. This was a willed act that caused survivors to have to go through the grief. Survivors are angry at the deceased for having put them through this death, as well as for having frustrated them during life.

Survivors may also feel angry if they feel they were tricked by the teenager. For example, a teenager said he was going to visit his friend but went out and shot himself in the park. Another teenager waited for her parents to leave the house for the evening and then took a large number of sleeping pills. A teenager may have used the threat of suicide to try to manipulate the parents, and then survivors may be even more angry. If they think the dead teenager intended them to suffer shame and guilt, they may be still angrier.

Helpers may listen to survivors' anger and encourage them to express their anger at the one who killed himself or herself. If survivors feel guilty for being angry at the teenager, helpers may remind them of what the teenager did that led them to be angry.

Adjustment

This stage helps you, as a survivor, restore yourself. You accept the fact that the teenager killed himself or herself, and you get on with living. If you've completed the other steps of grieving, it makes the adjustment easier, but still it may not occur automatically. You may need to give attention to it. For daily living, you put the suicide behind you, pick up the pieces, and start over again.

Adjusting to the death by suicide does not mean that the memories of the loved one must completely disappear. Healing is a process that goes from survivors having a bleeding wound to having a healed wound, and then to having a scar; and eventually even the scar becomes faint.

You need to talk about your teenager's death by suicide. Because of the social stigma against suicide or the horror of it, you may be hesitant to bring up the topic with friends, but you need to go through the difficulty and do it anyway. One teen whose best friend committed suicide said that in retrospect, he wished he had talked more with friends and family after it happened. A helpful beginning is to talk about how difficult it is to discuss the subject.

One way to make the adjustment is to identify the negative effects of the suicide on you personally and on your work, school, relationships, worship, and play. It is common to experience a "post-traumatic stress disorder." You may begin to have accidents, get sick, have irrational outbursts of sadness or anger, behave in unusual ways, start using drugs and alcohol, or take chances you didn't take before. You may withdraw socially; you may have disturbed relationships with your family members and friends. You may have dreams or fantasies of death and suicide, and so on. By identifying these kinds of reactions to the death, you may help prevent yourself from having additional negative reactions.

You may help yourself by writing in a journal of your

thoughts and writing poetry about your loved one's suicide. Keeping a journal or writing a poem is a way to express your feelings and also to put them aside. They are written on paper, and you can always read them again if you want to, but you can let the journal or poem contain your feelings and free you to think about other things.

One aspect of adjustment is that you eventually replace the loss with someone or something new. You are not disloyal to the deceased teenager if you shift your care and concern to someone new. Of course, you cannot replace the deceased teenager, but you find a way to fill the void left by his or her absence. Surviving parents may find other young people to nurture. They may have a niece or nephew live with them as she or he goes to college, become coaches of teenage sports teams, accept leadership of scout troops, make friends with a young adult couple, and so on. Surviving parents may develop new interests of their own, such as new hobbies or clubs and organizations. Some survivors decide to take an active role in campaigns against teenage suicide. The idea is that you intentionally do something new to fill the void. A surviving friend may find a new friend or a new interest to make up for the loss.

The death is a stress, but what stresses you may not be the death or suicide itself but your failure to express your feelings about it. Back up and check whether you have completed all the stages of the grieving process—cried enough, talked enough about your guilt and shame, and expressed enough of your anger at the deceased.

Help for Survivors

As a survivor of a suicide, you are not alone. Many people are in the position of having to cope with a teenage friend or family member having committed suicide. You may join groups of survivors of a child's death, such as the Compassionate Friends. You may find it helpful to go to individual or group psychotherapy.

There are many options open to you. By making the decision to heal, you are also paving the way toward moving on with your life.

Glossary

bias An adverse personal opinion of a person, group, or race of people.

denial In psychology, a defense mechanism of the mind to avoid facing a painful truth.

heterosexual Tending to be attracted to persons of the opposite sex.

homosexual Tending to be attracted to persons of the same sex.

identity The characteristics that distinguish one person from all others.

negotiating Discussing possible solutions of a dispute in an effort to reach a friendly settlement.

orientation The state of having a lasting attraction toward a particular sexual practice.

perspective The point of view from which one considers an object or an issue.

preoccupation The state of being absorbed by a subject to the exclusion of other matters.

reminiscing Recalling to mind a past event or experience.

statutory rape Sexual relations with a person beneath the legal age of consent.

stigma A mark of discredit or shame applied by society to the reputation of a person or group.

Where to Go for Help

Calling the Police

If you or someone you know is about to kill himself or herself, telephone 911.

Emergency Room of Hospital, Psychiatric Services

Most hospitals have an emergency room and have emergency psychiatric services available. Check with your family doctor or local hospital, if possible, before going to the hospital. Also, you may go with a friend or family member.

Telephone Hotlines or "Help-Lines" in Your City

Check the yellow pages under "Suicide."
Call 1-800-SVA-TEEN

Mental Health Professionals

There are school guidance counselors, school psychologists, psychiatrists and psychotherapists in your area.

Organizations:

American Association of Suicidology
4201 Connecticut Avenue, NW, Suite 310
Washington DC 20008
Tel: (202) 237-2280
Fax: (202) 237-2282
E-mail: medo117w@wonder.em.edc.gov

American Suicide Foundation
1045 Park Avenue, Suite 3C
New York, NY 10028
Tel: (212) 410-1111
Fax: (212) 410-0352
Web site: http://www.asfnet.org/

Canadian Mental Health Association
2610 Yonge Street
Toronto, ON M4S 2Z3
(416) 484-7750

Compassionate Friends
National Office
P.O. Box 3696 or Box 1347
Oak Brook, IL 60522-3696
(312) 990-0010 or (312) 232-5010
    Compassionate Friends is a self-help organization offering friendship and understanding to bereaved parents, siblings, grandparents, and so on.

Light for Life Foundation of America
P.O. Box 644
Westminster, CO 80030-0644
(303) 429-3530
Web site: http://www.yellowribbon.org
This site has references to many more sites.

National Committee on Youth Suicide Prevention
666 Fifth Avenue
New York, NY 10103
(212) 957-9292

SA/VE, Suicide Awareness, Voices of Education
Web site: http://www.save.org

Teen Suicide Prevention Task Force
P.O. Box 76463
Washington, DC 20013
(301) 627-5894

Youth Suicide National Center
1825 Eye Street NW, Suite 400
Washington, DC 20006
(202) 429-2016

For Further Reading

Axelrod, Toby. *Working Together Against Teen Suicide.* New York: The Rosen Publishing Group, Inc., 1996.

Copeland Lewis, Cynthia. *Teen Suicide: Too Young to Die.* Hillside, NJ: Enslow Publishers, Inc., 1994.

Gorman, J.. *The Essential Guide to Psychiatric Drugs.* New York: St. Martin's, 1995.

Klein, Wendy. *Drugs and Denial.* New York: The Rosen Publishing Group, Inc., 1998.

Marcus, E. (1996). *Why Suicide? Answers to 200 of the most frequently asked questions about suicide, attempted suicide and assisted suicide.* New York: HarperCollins, 1996.

Nelson, Richard E., Ph.D., and Galos, Judith C. *The Power to Prevent Suicide.* Minneapolis, MN: Free Spirit Publishing, Inc., 1994.

Packard, Gwen. *Coping with Stress.* New York: The Rosen Publishing Group, Inc., 1997.

Videotapes:

"Sometimes I Wonder If It's Worth It." A 30-minute videotape and guidebook on preventing teenage suicide for high school students and adults. (1986). Directed by Dale Linquist, M.Div. Produced by the Counseling Center of Southern Westchester, a branch of the Foundation for Religion and Mental Health, and by the Agency for Instructional Technology, Box A, Bloomington, Indiana 47402.

"When a Kid Is Gay." Since gay teens attempt suicide two to three times more often than heterosexual teens, it's important to understand the troubles gay youth face in order to help prevent their suicides. Produced by WGBH, Boston, duplication by: Color Guard Video, Box 416, Natick, MA 01760, (508) 655-2398. It may be also be ordered from UCC Conference Center, Box 2246, Framingham, MA 01701.

"Teens and Loss." Teens who lose family and friends go through great stress. One young woman talks about the loss of her sister through suicide. Produced by Saint Paul Bereavement Center, 189 Kernball Avenue, Staten Island, NY 10314, (718) 720-3363. It features Dr. Patrick Del Zoppo, Psy. D., a national leader in bereavement counseling.

Movies:
Night Mother
Moby Dick
Dead Poets' Society
Heathers

Index

differences, ethnic, 9–10
divorce, 12–13, 52

E
either-or thinking, 59–61, 69
energy
    lack of, 63
    restoring, 22
    suicidal, 74
evaluation, psychiatric, 83, 86

F
faith, as force for life, 97–98
family
    influence of, 50–53
    issues, 12–14, 52
    relations with, 47–58
feelings
    change in, 34–36
    dealing with, 37–46
    positive, 88–90
filibustering, 39
Freud, Sigmund, 108
friends
    as force for life, 90–93
    influence of, 49
    plan for six, 94
    relations with, 47–58
frustration, 38, 48, 66, 74
    with self, 34–36
functioning, as force for life, 95–96

G
grieving, stages of, 102–116

guilt, feelings of, 34, 37, 41, 44–46
    about a death, 55–56, 102, 107, 110–112

H
heaven vs. hell, 62–63
help, getting, 80–81, 84–87
Hemingway, Ernest, 58
hopelessness, 21, 29, 74
hospitalization, 86–87
hotline, 3, 15
homosexuality, 7–8, 72–73

I
identity, 9
    gender, 6
    sexual, 7
incest, 13–14
insomnia, 31–32, 57

J
journal, keeping, 67–68, 115

L
life
    enjoying, 4, 71–72
    forces for, 88–100
loss, of loved one, 53–55
love, abundance view of, 89

M
marasmus, 68
medication, 83, 86, 87
merry-go-round, getting off, 20

123

DATE DUE

~~		~~NOV 3 0~~	

362.28
Mur   Murphy, James M.
         Coping with teen suicide